CAPTIVES BOUND IN CHAINS MADE FREE BY CHRIST

By Thomas Doolittle

COPYRIGHT INFORMATION

Captives Bound in Chains Made Free by Christ, by Thomas Doolittle
Edited and updated by C. Matthew McMahon and Therese B. McMahon
Transcribed by Joel Swearington

Copyright © 2012, 2017 by Puritan Publications and A Puritan's Mind

Some language and grammar has been updated from the original manuscript. Any change in wording or punctuation has not changed the intent or meaning of the original author(s), and has been made to aid the modern reader.

Published by Puritan Publications
A Ministry of A Puritan's Mind
Crossville, TN
www.apuritansmind.com
www.puritanpublications.com

All rights reserved. No part of this publication may be reproduced, stored in a retrieval system or transmitted in any form by any means, electronic, mechanical, photocopy, recording or otherwise, without the prior permission of the publisher, except as provided by USA copyright law.

Hardback Print Edition, 2012
Paperback Print Edition, 2017
Electronic Edition, 2012
Manufactured in the United States of America.

Hardback ISBN: 978-1-938721-59-5
Paperback ISBN: 978-1-62663-278-3
eISBN: 978-1-938721-58-8

TABLE OF CONTENTS

MEET THOMAS DOOLITTLE 5
INTRODUCTORY LETTER 11
CHAPTER 1: THE TEXT OPENED 16
CHAPTER 2: THE DEVIL'S CAPTIVES 24
CHAPTER 3: THE FIRST LINK – IGNORANCE 37
CHAPTER 4: THE SECOND LINK – PREJUDICE 41
CHAPTER 5: THE THIRD LINK – LOVE OF THE WORLD
.... 67
CHAPTER 6: THE FOURTH LINK – PRESUMPTION 73
CHAPTER 7: THE FIFTH LINK – DESPAIR 103
CHAPTER 8: THE 6th AND 7th LINKS – MORALITY AND RELIGIOUS DUTIES 109
CHAPTER 9: THE 8th, 9th AND 10th LINKS 114
CHAPTER 10: CAPTIVITY BY SATAN WORSE THAN CAPTIVITY IN SLAVERY BY MEN 122
CHAPTER 11: FREEDOM IN CHRIST 134
CHAPTER 12: APPLICATION AND USES 151

CAPTIVES
BOUND IN
CHAINS
Made FREE by
CHRIST
THEIR
SURETY

OR,
The Misery of Graceless Sinners, and
Their Recovery by Christ their Savior.

By Thomas Doolittle

"The Lord called you in righteousness, and will hold you by the hand, and will keep you, and give you as a covenant for the people, a light for the Gentiles, To open the eyes that are blind, yes, to bring out the prisoners from the dungeon, from the prison those who sit in darkness,"
(Isa. 42:6-7).

"That you may say to the prisoners, 'Go forth,' to them that are in darkness, 'Show yourselves,'" (Isa. 49:9).

"As for you also, by the blood of your covenant,
I have sent forth your prisoners out of the waterless pit. Return to your stronghold, O prisoners of hope; today I declare that I will restore to you double," (Zech. 9:11-12).

LONDON.
Printed by *A.M.* for *Tho. Parkhurst*, at the
Bible and three towns in *Cheapside* near Mercer's
Chapel, and at the Bible on *London Bridge*, 1674.

MEET THOMAS DOOLITTLE
Edited by C. Matthew McMahon, Ph.D., Th.D.

Thomas Doolittle (1632–1707), nonconformist tutor and preacher, third son of Anthony Doolittle, a glover, was born at Kidderminster in 1632 or the latter half of 1631. While at the grammar school of his native town, he heard Richard Baxter preach as lecturer (appointed April 5, 1641) the sermons afterwards published as "The Saint's Everlasting Rest" (1653). These discourses produced his conversion. Placed with a country attorney, he scrupled at copying writings on Sunday, and went home determined not to follow the law. Baxter encouraged him to enter the ministry. He was admitted as a sizar at Pembroke Hall, Cambridge, on June 7, 1649, being then "17 *annos natus*." He could not, therefore, have been born in 1630, as stated in his "memoirs." The source of the error is that another Thomas, son of William and Jane Doolittle, was baptized at Kidderminster on Oct. 20, 1630. His tutor was William Moses, afterwards ejected from the mastership of Pembroke. Doolittle graduated with an M.A. at Cambridge. Leaving the university for London, he became popular as a preacher, and in preference to other candidates was chosen (in 1653) as their pastor by the parishioners of St. Alphage, London Wall. The living is described as sequestered in Rastrick's list as quoted by Palmer, but James Halsey, D.D., the deprived rector, had been dead twelve or thirteen years. Doolittle received Presbyterian ordination. During the nine years of his incumbency he fully sustained his popularity. On the passing of the Uniformity Act (1662) he "upon the whole thought it his duty to be a nonconformist." He was poor; the day after his farewell sermon a parishioner made him a welcome present of 20£. A residence had been built for Doolittle, but it appears to have been private property; it neither went to his successor, Matthew Fowler, D.D., nor did Doolittle continue to enjoy it. He removed to Moorfields and opened a boarding-school, which succeeded so well that he took a larger house in Bunhill Fields, where he was assisted by Thomas Vincent, ejected from St. Mary Magdalene, Milk Street.

In the year of the plague (1665) Doolittle and his pupils removed to Woodford Bridge, near Chigwell, close to Epping Forest, Vincent remaining behind. Returning to London in 1666, Doolittle was one of the nonconformist ministers who, in defiance of the law, erected preaching-places when churches were lying in ruins after the great fire. His first meeting-house (probably a wooden structure) was in Bunhill Fields, and here he was undisturbed. But when he transferred his congregation to a large and substantial building (the first of the kind in London, if not in England) which he had erected in Mugwell (now Monkwell) Street, the authorities set the law in motion against him. The lord mayor amicably endeavored to persuade him to desist from preaching; he declined. On the following Saturday about midnight his door was broken open by a force sent to arrest him. He escaped over a wall, and intended to preach next day. From this he was dissuaded by his friends, one of whom (Thomas Sare, ejected from Rudford, Gloucestershire) took his place in the pulpit. The sermon was interrupted by the appearance of a body of troops. As the preacher stood his ground "the officer bid his men to fire." "Shoot, if you please," was the reply. There was an considerable uproar, but no arrests were made. The meeting-house, however, was taken possession of in the name of the king, and for some time was utilized as a lord mayor's chapel. On the indulgence of March 15, 1672 Doolittle took out a license for his meeting-house. The original document, dated April 2, hangs in Dr. Williams's library. The meeting-house is described as "a certain roome adjoining to ye dwelling-house of Thomas Doelitle in Mugwell Street." Doolittle owned the premises, but he now resided in Islington, where his school had developed into an academy for "university learning." When Charles II (March 8, 1673) broke the seal of his declaration of indulgence, thus invalidating the licenses granted under it, Doolittle conducted his academy with great caution at Wimbledon. His biographers represent this removal as a consequence of the passing (it may have been an instance of the enforcing) of the Five Miles Act (in 1665). At Wimbledon he had a narrow escape from arrest. He returned to Islington before 1680, but in 1683 he was again dislodged. He removed to Battersea (where his goods were seized), and then to Clapham. These migrations destroyed his academy, but not before he had contributed to the education of some men of notation. Matthew Henry, Samuel Bury, Thomas Emlyn, and Edmund Calamy, D.D., were among his pupils. Two of his students, John Kerr, M.D., and Thomas Rowe, achieved distinction as nonconformist tutors.

The academy was at an end in 1687, when Doolittle lived at St. John's Court, Clerkenwell, and had Calamy a second time under his care for some months as a boarder. Until the death of his wife he still continued to receive students for the ministry, but apparently not more than one at a time. His last pupil was Nathaniel Humphreys.

The Toleration Act of 1689 left Doolittle free to resume his services at Mugwell Street, preaching twice every Sunday and lecturing on Wednesdays. Vincent, his assistant, had died in 1678; later he had as assistants his pupil, John Mottershead (removed to Ratcliff Cross), his son, Samuel Doolittle (removed to Reading), and Daniel Wilcox, who succeeded him. Emlyn's son and biographer says of Doolittle that he was "a very worthy and diligent divine, yet was not eminent for compass of knowledge or depth of thought." This estimate is borne out by his "Body of Divinity," a painstaking and prolix expansion of the assembly's shorter catechism, more remarkable for its conscientiousness and unction than for its intellectual grasp. His private covenant of personal religion (Nov. 18, 1693) occupies six closely printed folio pages. He had long suffered from stone and other infirmities, but his last illness was very brief. He preached and catechized with great vigor on Sunday, May 18, took to his bed in the latter part of the week, lay for two days unconscious, and died on May 24, 1707. He was the last survivor of the London ejected clergy. Six portraits of Doolittle have been engraved; one represents him in his own hair "ætatis suæ 52;" another, older and in a bushy wig, has less expression. The latter was engraved by James Caldwall for the first edition of Palmer (1775), from a painting in the possession of S. Sheaf or Sheafe, Doolittle's grandson; in the second edition a worthless substitute is given. Doolittle married in 1653, shortly after his ordination; his wife died in 1692. Of his family of three sons and six daughters, all except a daughter, were dead in 1723.

Doolittle's twenty publications are carefully enumerated at the close of the "Memoirs" (1723), probably by Jeremiah Smith. They begin with (1) "Sermon on Assurance in the Morning Exercise at Cripplegate," 1661, 4to, and consist of sermons and devotional treatises, of which (2) "A Treatise concerning the Lord's Supper," 1665, 12mo (portrait by R. White), and (3) "A Call to Delaying Sinners," 1683, 12mo, went through many editions. His latest work published in his lifetime was (4) "The Saint's Convoy to, and Mansions in Heaven," 1698, 8vo. Posthumous was (5) "A Complete Body of Practical Divinity," *etc.* 1723, fol. (the editors say this volume was the product of his Wednesday catechetical lectures, "catechising was his special excellency and delight;" the list of subscribers includes several clergymen of the established church). One of his most vibrant sermon series, later turned into a tract, was "Captives Bound in Chains Made Free by Christ Their Surety", 1674. Also, his work "The Swearer Silenced" in 1674 was made popular.

For Further Study:

[*Funeral Sermon* by Daniel Williams, D.D., 1707; Calamy's *Account*, 1713, pp. 52, 331; Continuation, 1727, pp. 75, 506; Hist. of my own Life, 2nd edit. 1830, i. 105, 138, ii. 78; Walker's *Sufferings*, 1714, pt. ii. p. 171; Tong's *Life of Matthew Henry*, 1716; *Memoirs* prefixed to *Body of Divinity*, 1723; *Memoir of T. Emlyn* prefixed to his *Works*, 4th edit. 1746, i. 7; *Protestant Dissenters'* Mag. 1799, p. 392; Palmer's *Nonconf. Memorial*, 2nd edit. 1802, i. 86; Toulmin's *Hist. View of Prot. Diss.* 1814, pp. 237, 584; Granger's *Biog. Hist. of England*, 1824, v. 67; Lee's *Diaries and Letters of P. Henry*, 1882, p. 334, &c.; Jeremy's *Presbyterian Fund*, 1885, pp. 7, 12, &c.; information from records of Presbyterian Board, by W.D. Jeremy; extract from Pembroke College Records per the Rev. C.E. Searle, D.D., and from parish register, Kidderminster, per Mr. R. Grove.]

INTRODUCTORY LETTER

To the *Congregation* to whom this book was first preached in sermons to, and to whom these original sermons belong, whether bond or free.

Dearly Beloved, and longed-for, my joy and crown:

The serious consideration of the immortality of your souls, the captivity of many among you to Satan and to sin, the eternity you are approaching to, the necessity of being made free from spiritual bondage, the shortness and uncertainty of your abode on earth, your capacity of being set at liberty by Christ (while you are on this side of the grave), the impossibility of redemption and deliverance or sinful and hellish thralldom after death, moved me at first to preach these sermons on this subject to your ears, and now to present them to your eyes, hoping that as the having of them in your hands to view what has been said to you will be a help to your memories. They also are a means to continue further and increase that sense of the evil of *soul-captivity*, that sorrow that you had when you were captives to Satan so long, and those desires to change your master, and have your fetters knocked off, and be brought into the liberty of the sons of God, by Christ the Son of God, all which many of you (through the grace of God, for his work it was, and its glory is due alone to him) manifested and declared, not only in your earnest desires for God's sake, and for Christ's sake, that the congregation, if they had any love for, or pity to miserable enthralled souls, would solemnly and fervently pray to God, that the chains of sin, by which you had been held, might now be cut, and the bonds broke. But also in your private converse with me, which is here related (the Lord knows) not that I may be accounted anything (for I know that I am nothing), or that I put any great esteem on anything that I can do. For I do judge myself as to gifts or graces or both, to be the meanest desire employed in the work of the Lord, and service of immortal souls. But that if God is pleased to work by a weak and silly man, the glory might be ascribed unto him.

Man at first was made the most noble and most excellent creature of all God's visible works, endued with such powers that he was capable of knowing, loving, and enjoying God his maker as his happiness, felicity, and end, created free from sin and corruption, and free from sorrow and affliction, though not free from temptation, nor from a possibility of losing his freedom. Yet he had a power and a liberty to have continued in that condition, without any necessity of co-action to depart from it.

But this free and noble creature assaulted and set on by the crafty and malicious serpent, and left to the freedom of his own will, was prevailed with and overcome by Satan, to transgress the Law of his Maker, and violate his covenant, proved an apostate, and turned rebel against God that gave him his being, and that good condition in which he was created, who by the abusing of his liberty lost his freedom, and brought himself and all his posterity into an estate of slavery and bondage, out of which he was no way able to help himself.

Man lying in this pitiful plight, in this forlorn, miserable and deplorable condition, the God of grace and mercy (of his mere grace and mercy) did commiserate, seek after him, find him out, and made known a way of redemption for him, even by the incarnation, passion, and crucifixion of his own son, which he did more and more clearly in several ages discover to the captivated children of enthralled Adam. Where he provided no redeemer for fallen angels, but where they fell, there they lie, bound in chains of darkness, without hope of help, or possibility of recovery to all eternity. Behold, you captive sons of men, here is a remedy for you, but not for devils. For God did not send his Son to take on him the nature of angels, but the seed of Abraham, and that when the apostatizing angels sinned, and were falling down to hell, Christ did not take hold on them. But on man (when by reason of sin he was tumbling and sinking into everlasting misery) he took hold, and snatched him from the flames of eternal burnings, from the curse of the law, and from the intolerable wrath of an angry and provoked God.

This God and Savior that foresaw your thralldom and bondage, did from all eternity agree and covenant between themselves in this way of redemption to afford you succor and relief, that Christ should become your surety, and be bound for you that were bound, and died for you that should have died eternally, and set you at liberty by paying down a valuable ransom for you, of which you should be partakers. This will only happen if you turn from sin to God, from Satan to his Son, heartily consenting to take him for your Lord-Redeemer, for your Prophet, Priest, and King, to rule, instruct, sanctify and save you, resigning yourselves and all you have and are to him, preferring him before all, loving him above all, believing on him, and obeying of him sincerely, constantly, and universally, without partiality, and sinful, secret reservations. And if you do not like him, and do not receive deliverance from your bonds and fetters on these conditions, you must lie and perish in your chains of sin and guilt forever.

This is that Redeemer that is preached, published, and tendered to you. This is he, and he alone that can make you free, and if *he* does, you shall be free indeed. Receive him as he is offered, and deliverance and salvation will come to you. Refuse him, slight him, or neglect him, and you are captives without ransom *irrecoverably*. All of you by nature were in this state of spiritual captivity, and all of you are now bond or free. For as there are but two places in the other world appointed by God to be receptacles of men's souls, namely, heaven and hell, so in this world there are but two sorts of men (so distinguished by their spiritual state): *captives* or *free*, the one continuing so, so shall be plunged into hell, and the other shall be possessed of heaven. Under which of these you are comprehended, you may be helped to discern, if you will read, consider, search, and pray. If you find yourselves yet captives, to know your misery, and the chains by which you are bound, and how to get them off, read the former part of this little book. If free, to enflame your hearts with love to your Redeemer and Surety, that paid the ransom for you. And learn how you are engaged to hearty and everlasting thankfulness for his mercy towards you, and to express it by holy walking while you live, consult the latter part of this treatise. In all which I have endeavored to use plain speech, avoiding hard words, and difficult terms, as also controversies that might have been brought into this subject, concerning the power and will of man, concerning the satisfaction of Christ, and such like, contenting myself with what may suit the end I aimed at in preaching of them, the awakening of the conscience of captive sinners that are fast asleep in their fetters and bonds of iniquity, and the bringing of the more ignorant to sight and sense of their necessity of deliverance by Christ. (As for the more knowing, let them read the works of men of more knowledge.) For if I may by any means help the weak and ignorant, that cannot understand the elaborate works of the more judicious, I shall account it a singular mercy. For if I could, I do not dare usually, when I am to speak in the name of God to immortal souls, soar aloft above the capacity of the meanest. The strong might stoop to the plainness of wholesome words, when the weak and ignorant cannot come up to the understanding of what is more sublime, though rude and undigested matter does not become the place of any that stands to speak to people going to another world, about things of everlasting concernment. Yet I judge that he shall have but little comfort another day, that stands and speaks one word for Christ, and two or ten for himself, a little to set forth Christ, and much to set forth his own parts. If any look for such things here, that they may not lose their labor, let me desire them to lay it by, for you will not find it. But that this in its plain dress and style, without all pomp of words, being read by you, or any others, might be to the profit of you or them, is the desire, and shall be the prayers of him that *is*,

Yours for the service of your souls,
THOMAS DOOLITTLE
March 18, 1674.

CHAPTER 1: THE TEXT OPENED

Containing the Explanation of the Text

"The Spirit of the Lord God is on me, because the Lord has anointed me to preach good tidings to the meek. He has sent me to bind up the broken-hearted, to proclaim liberty to the captives, and the opening of the prison to them that are bound," (Isa. 61:1).

These words, though true of the prophet Isaiah, yet have a principal reference to Christ, who, going into the synagogue on the Sabbath day, chose these words for his text, and preached on it to the admiration of his hearers, (Luke 4:18). And he applied these words to himself, as chiefly intended, (Luke 4:21). Other holy men of God had the Spirit of the Lord on them, and it was imparted to them, by which they spoke, (1 Peter 1:11; 2 Peter 1:21). But Christ had this in a more eminent manner and measure, "And the Spirit of the Lord shall rest on him, the Spirit of wisdom and understanding, the Spirit of counsel and might, the Spirit of knowledge and of the fear of the Lord," (Isa. 11:2). "Behold, my servant whom I uphold, my elect in whom my soul delights, I have put my spirit on him, and he shall bring forth judgment to the Gentiles," (Isa. 42:1). Yes, Christ had the Spirit more abundantly than all others, "For he whom God has sent, speaks the words of God, for God does not give the Spirit by measure to him," (Job 3:34). All believers are anointed of God, have received a spiritual and holy unction in some measure of sanctifying grace. "Now he who establishes us with you in Christ, and has anointed us, is God," (2 Cor. 1:21). "But you have an unction from the Holy one, and you know all things," (1 John 2:20). "But the anointing which you have received of him abides in you, and you do not need any man to teach you," (the grounds of religion which you have already learned, or any new doctrines which you have not already received), "but as the same anointing teaches you of all things," (needful to be known in order to salvation, or to preserve you from being deceived or drawn away by false teachers), "and is truth, and is no lie, and even as it has taught you, you shall abide in him," (1 John 2:27).

Besides this anointing common to all God's people, there is a more special unction by which certain persons chosen and called of God to holy employment especially are fitted and qualified with gifts and graces for the better discharge of their office, in former times typified by material unctions, "And he poured of the anointing oil on Aaron's head, and anointed him to sanctify him," (Lev. 8:12). But Christ was anointed in a larger manner and fuller measure than any other, being chosen and called and appointed by God to the office of mediator between God and man, which no other was capable of, or fitted for. "Therefore God, your God, has anointed you with the oil of gladness above your fellows," (Psa. 45:7). Christ had a fullness of abundance, "In whom are hid all the treasures of wisdom and knowledge," (Col. 2:3). "For in him dwells all the fullness of the Godhead bodily," (Col. 2:9). And Christ had a fullness of redundancy that flows over to his people. Like the ointment on the head of Aaron that ran down to the skirts of his garments, (Psa. 133:2), so there is a conveyance of grace and spiritual gifts from Christ to his members, who is like a fountain, that though it overflows, yet ever-flows, sends forth its streams, and yet is still full. "For it pleased the Father, that in him should all fullness dwell," (Col. 1:19). "And of his fullness we have all received, and grace for grace," (John 1:16). As from the fullness of sin for sin, so from the fullness of grace in Christ the second Adam, all God's people receive grace for grace.

Christ was in this way anointed (to preach good tidings to the meek). When man had sinned, sad tidings were brought to him, "Cursed is the ground for your sake." Tidings of toil and labor, tidings of death, and of the evils contained in the threatening, tidings of wrath and sore displeasure from a provoked God. Yet God himself did preach the first tidings of a Savior to lost man, (Gen. 3:15). When the Lord sent a message to Israel by Moses, that "because they were a stiff-necked people, he would come into the midst of them, and consume them," these were evil tidings, and cause of morning, (Exod. 33:4). The Prophet was sent to Jeroboam with heavy tidings, (1 Kings 14:6). But when man was in a lost condition, the discoveries of a Savior were the best and gladdest tidings that could be brought unto him. If God had said to man, "I will make you rich, but I will not forgive your sins. You shall live long in the world, but not eternally with me in heaven. You will live on earth all your days in ease and pleasure, but after death in pain and torments," these would have been *heavy* tidings. But for God to say and send to lost man this news, you have undone yourself, but I will help you. You have lost your soul, your God, your happiness, but I will restore you. I will give and send my Son to seek and to save lost sinners. Was this not *joyful* tidings? God sent his prophets to publish these tidings to the world, (Isa. 52:7). And apostles came with these glad tidings, (Acts 13:32). And angels, "The angel said, do not fear, behold, I bring you good tidings of great joy, which shall be to all the people," (Luke 2:10). But these tidings were not only brought by prophets, apostles, and angels, but by Christ himself. "He went through every village and city, preaching and showing the glad

Chapter 1: The Text Opened

tidings of the kingdom of God," (Luke 8:1). David said of Ahimaaz, "he is a good man, and he brings good tidings," (2 Sam. 18:27). But Christ we may say, is a good Savior, and brings good, the best tidings that ever were reported to the children of men. And when Christ returned to heaven, he has given commission to his ministers to preach and publish the same tidings. As Cushi said running in haste, "Tidings, my lord the king," (2 Sam. 18:31). So we come to poor sinners, saying "Tidings to you poor, perishing sinners, tidings. Tidings from God, tidings from heaven." What? What are they? Are they glad tidings? May sinners expect any glad tidings? Tell us, O tell us, what are these tidings that you bring? What are they? *Christ a Savior for lost sinners. Christ a physician for sick and wounded sinners. Pardon for the guilty sinner. Peace for the troubled sinner. Life to the condemned sinner. Heaven for the hell-deserving sinner. These, these are tidings that are brought to you.* "O how beautiful are the feet of them that preach the gospel of peace, and bring glad tidings of good things," (Rom. 10:15). But do you bring these tidings to great sinners of a scarlet dye? Yes, if you repent, and turn to God, and receive Christ on gospel terms for Lord and Savior, here are tidings in the gospel brought by Christ himself of pardon and salvation, (Job 3:16). But what if we do not? Has Christ brought any sad and heavy tidings? Yes, truly, as you may read, "He that does not believe shall be damned," (Mark 16:16). It was sad tidings when news was brought that the ark was lost, (1 Sam. 4:19). But O what heavy tidings will it be to the refusers of mercy, to the slighters of Christ and his grace, when it shall be told them, "Now your souls are forever lost, and God and Christ is forever lost, and heaven's happiness is forever lost." In a word, Christ came principally to preach good tidings to poor sinners, but yet he also brings terrible tidings to the impenitent and unbelieving.

He has sent me to bind up the broken-hearted. When man by sin had broken covenant with God, he broke the peace with God, and all mankind were broken in Adam, and proved bankrupt. And though all are broken by sin, yet few are broken for sin, all of us put up broken duties, but few of us have broken hearts. Many are broken in their estates through poverty, and many men's bodies are broken through age and sickness. But yet their hearts do not break for their sin. But this is the comfort of broken-hearted sinners, that Christ himself was sent to bind you up, to dress and to heal your wounded broken hearts. Surgeons may set and bind broken and disjointed bones, but Christ alone can set, and bind, and give ease to broken *hearts*. When by sinning you break the commands of God, he is highly offended and provoked. "But the soul that does anything presumptuously, the same reproaches the Lord, and that soul shall be cut off from among his people, because he has despised the word of the Lord, and has broken his commandments. That soul shall be utterly cut off, and his iniquity shall be on him," (Num. 15:30-31). But when by sorrowing and repenting your heart is broken because you have broken the commands of God, he is well-pleased with you. "The sacrifices of God are a broken spirit; a broken and contrite heart, O God, you will not despise," (Psa. 51:17). When you broke the command of God, you despised God, (2 Sam. 12:9). But when your heart is broken for your sin, God will not despise your broken-heart, but God himself will come and bind and heal you," (Psa. 147:3). "He will come and revive your contrite spirit," (Isa. 47:15). "He will come and be nigh unto you, and will save you," (Psa. 34:18). The sum of all is this: if you are broken for your sins, you shall not die of the wounds made by sin in your soul.

To proclaim liberty to the captives and the opening of the prison to them that are bound. This might partly refer to the temporal deliverance by Cyrus from the Babylonian captivity, but chiefly denotes the spiritual freedom from the bondage and thralldom of Satan and sin by Christ.

In these words you may observe,

1. A choice and precious privilege. Bondage and thralldom is a sore evil, liberty as great a good. But the spiritual bondage and slavery of the soul to Satan and to sin is far worse than corporal bondage, than Turkish slavery. Therefore, spiritual liberty by Christ is far beyond (in its excellency and desirableness) any outward deliverance from bodily bondage.

2. The persons that this privilege is for. For those that are captives. The blessings and privileges that sinners have by Christ are suitable to their necessity, restoring of sight to the blind, limbs to the lame, health to the sick, ease to the pained, and liberty to the captive, are all seasonable and suitable mercies.

3. The publishing, declaring, and making it known, by way of proclamation. The great God that might have kept sinners in bonds forever, and in prison forever, does pass an act of grace, and sent his own Son into the world, to proclaim liberty to spiritual bondmen. Proclamation has been made by Christ himself, that prisoners may be released, that those that are bound in chains may have their fetters knocked off, and such as have been taken captive by the devil, the common enemy of man's salvation, may be set at liberty. And the ministers of the gospel are given by Christ, and sent by him as the *heralds* of the great King of heaven and earth, to proclaim pardon to the penitent, healing to the wounded, ease to the burdened, liberty to the captives. Christ did this in person in the days of his flesh on earth, (Job 7:37). And now the ministers of Christ proclaim the same things in Christ's stead, (2 Cor. 5:18-20). Cyrus, King of Persia, put forth a proclamation throughout all his kingdom to give free liberty to the captive Jews to go back to Jerusalem, to build the house of the Lord, saying, "Who is there among you of all his people, the Lord his God be with him, and let him go up," (2 Chron. 36:22-23). So the Lord, the King of nations, has made a proclamation, and put it in writing, and commands his servants to go up and proclaim, "Return, you sinners, to me, and I will not cause my anger to fall on you, for I am merciful, says the Lord God, and I will not keep anger forever," (Jer. 3:12). I might be angry with you, as long as I am God, but if you will repent and turn, I will not. I could pour out my wrath on you forever. But if you will forsake your wicked ways, "Iniquity shall not be your ruin," (Ezek. 18:30-31; Isa. 55:1-7). Who is there among you, that are weary of the service of sin? You might be received into better service, and have a better reward. Who is there among you that are weary of your chains and fetters? Be but willing, and you shall be freed from them. Who is there among you that has lain long in the jail of Satan, in the filthy, dark dungeon of an unconverted state? Behold, Christ is come to open the prison doors. "Go forth, come away, sinners, come away," not only one by one, which yet would be a matter of joy, to see one Lord's day, and another on another Lord's day to come out of prison. But since the prison doors are open, and Christ is come to knock off your fetters, "Come, come away by companies, come, come away in numbers." Come! Who steps out of the prison first? Who would not? I think I see one, he is unwilling to come forth, and another does not regard it. What ails you, sirs? Is a dungeon so delicate that you are unwilling to leave it? What ails you? Sinner! Are you yourself, your own man? Are you in your right mind? You are worse than mad, that will not put off chains of iron, for chains of gold, that will not leave a prison for a palace, thick darkness for marvelous, glorious, shining light. Do you think, if all the prison doors in the land were opened, and proclamation made, that whoever would might have free liberty to go forth, that any would remain there? O, why then are the devils prisoners, and those that are captives to their lusts, the only persons that like and love their bondage? That might have deliverance, but will not? But give yourself the labor to hear what shall be said of the miserable condition of these captives, and afterwards I hope you will be wiser for yourself, for your soul, than to refuse spiritual freedom, and to choose your chains and fetters.

CHAPTER 2:
THE DEVIL'S CAPTIVES

The Doctrine. Showing also in what unconverted men are resembled to captives.

I. **DOCTRINE**. Unconverted men are the devil's captives, being fast bound with the chains and bonds of their own iniquity and sin.

Presently after the creation of man, there was a spiritual war, conflict, and combat between man and the devil. The place where this war began was paradise, in which fight the devil overcame, and did prevail, not only against our first parents, but their posterity also. Then was man first carried captive and taken prisoner by the devil, and remains so until he is rescued, redeemed, and delivered by Jesus Christ the Captain of our salvation. So wicked men are said to be "taken captive by the devil at his will," (2 Tim. 2:26), and keeps them in a peaceable, quiet subjection to him, (Luke 11:21), and dwells, works, and rules in their hearts, (Eph. 2:2). The heart of an unregenerate sinner is the devil's garrison, fort, and stronghold, where he sits, and acts, and commands like an usurping tyrant. And the poor sinner yields obedience to him without opposition or resistance. So are they also said to be "bound fast in the bond of iniquity and sin," (Acts 8:23), and are "the servants of sin, and slaves to their own corruption and lusts," (Rom. 6:16), and "serve diverse lusts," (Titus 3:3-5), and are "the servants of corruption," who, becoming overcome by Satan and by sin, are brought into bondage by them, (2 Peter 2:19).

In these particulars following, it will appear that uncoverted, graceless men are captives and bondmen to Satan and to sin.

1. *Captives and bondmen are disarmed.* Their weapons and armor of defense are taken from them, that they are not able to make resistance against those by whom they are taken captives and prisoners. Sirs, the enemies of your souls are,

1. *Powerful enemies.* Called principalities and powers, (Eph. 6:12). Compared to a lion for their mighty strength, (1 Peter 5:8). And what is a naked and unarmed man against a powerful enemy?

2. *Political as well as powerful.* Strength and stratagems, power and policy make an enemy very formidable. Here Satan is compared to a serpent for his subtlety and craft, (Gen. 3:1). And the old serpent, that by the experience of many thousand years has obtained greater still in his cursed art of tempting and destroying the souls of men, (Rev. 12:9). And if he beguiled our first parents through his subtlety, when they were perfect in wisdom and knowledge, (2 Cor. 11:3). O, what danger the soul of a sinner is now in, when he has become not only weak, but foolish also! (Titus 3:3). The devil has a thousand methods, and stratagems, and devices to entrap and to ensnare your souls, of which you read, (2 Cor. 2:11).

3. *The enemies of your souls are many and numerous.* It is not one sin, nor one temptation, nor one devil that set themselves to bring your soul's damnation. But many devils and many lusts against one poor unarmed sinner. A whole legion of devils entered into one poor man, (Luke 8:30). So not one only, but many devils might busy themselves to ruin and undo your soul.

4. *The enemies of your souls are malicious as well as numerous.* When the devil was dispossessed of his first estate, he envied the happiness of man, and most maliciously set himself to endeavor that man might not forever enjoy what he

and his angels with him had forever lost. The devil is often called "the wicked one," (Matt. 3:19; Eph. 6:16; 1 John 2:13; 5:18). But the original word signifies something more than barely wicked, a *troublesome one*, or the *malicious one*, for the devil through his malice is the troubler of men, being studious and desirous to do men mischief, especially as to their souls and everlasting concerns.

5. *The enemies of your souls are invisible*, because they are spiritual wickednesses, (Eph. 6:12). An enemy not seen, nor discerned, is the more dangerous; that tempts you oftentimes and you do not perceive him, that wounds you but you do not discern him, setting on you secretly, and because invisibly, before you are aware of him.

6. *They are indefatigable or unwearied enemies.* Satan has been employed in this work of tempting and destroying souls for some thousand years, and yet he is not weary, so as to desist, to this day. This work he began but a very little after the beginning of the world and this he will without growing weary carry on to the end of the world. While there are men out of heaven and hell, he will not leave off his soul-destroying study and endeavors. And when on earth he shall have no more to tempt then he shall torment them forever that by temptations he has got to hell. So like a restless spirit he is always *going to and fro in the earth, and walking up and down in it*, going from one person to another, from one house to another, to and fro, backwards and forwards, up and down, here and there, as one that cannot be at quiet without his prey, (Job 1:7; 2:2). "He walks about, seeking whom he may devour," (1 Peter 5:8), seeking not to devour souls one by one, but if it may be by whole families, by whole parishes, by whole kingdoms and

nations, and so he does to many in the world, where the gospel and a Savior has not been heard of.

So are graceless sinners like a company of poor unarmed prisoners in the midst of *many, malicious, powerful, political, and unwearied enemies* that do design nothing less than the damnation of your soul, the loss, the eternal God, that design nothing less than to bring you to a place of torment, to a fiery furnace, to a lake of brimstone, to a place of utter darkness, where there shall be weeping, and wailing, and gnashing of teeth, woe and lamentation, shriekings and howlings, and bitter cries forever and ever. O, how should it pity us to see these poor naked unarmed sinners surrounded by such mighty enemies, carrying them captives to a place of eternal separation from God, and Christ, and angels, and all the saints of God, to see them going to the slaughterhouse of hell, and to the place of dreadful execution.

Poor captivated souls! Are you in this way in the hands of your enemies, and not one piece of spiritual armor to safeguard yourselves? Captives lie at the mercy of those whose slaves they are. But Satan has no such thing as mercy or pity to the souls of men. Malice enough, but no mercy. Cruelty enough, but no favor. If God should have no mercy for you, the devil will have none. Except the God of mercy, and pity, and patience had restrained the enemies of your souls, they would have dragged you down to the bottomless pit long before this day. There is *armor of proof* against those that have taken you captive, and you do not have the *armor of God*. But this is your misery, you do not have one piece of it, neither girdle of truth, nor the breastplate of righteousness, nor the helmet of salvation, and though you may have the sword of the Spirit, the word of God in your hands, yet you do not know how to use it against the assaults of your spiritual adversaries. Think then of this, captives are naked and unarmed men.

2. *Captives lose the riches they had, when taken captives.* Though they were rich before, yet they are made poor, and are stripped of all. If a rich merchant at sea has many goods in a ship, costly jewels, precious pearls, and is taken prisoner, and carried captive, he is spoiled of all, and loses all. Man at first was exceedingly rich, rich in the knowledge of God, rich in love and likeness to God. The holiness of man was his riches, the enjoyment of God was his riches, the spiritual endowments of man at first were not to be valued with the gold of Ophir, with the precious onyx or the sapphire. Gold and crystal could not equal them, they were not to be exchanged for jewels of fine gold, the topaz of Ethiopia could not equal them, neither were they to be valued with pure gold, coral, or pearls were not worthy to be mentioned with them, for their price was above rubies, as Job sets for the excellency of wisdom, (Job 28:15-20). But when man was overcome by the devil and taken captive by him, he was spoiled of all, all was taken from him, that he became miserably poor, lost his knowledge of God, the image of God, the favor or God, communion with God, the gracious comfortable presence of God, his abode in paradise. And though before he was lord of all, and had dominion over all inferior creatures, yet being captivated by the devil, he lost his right to all, and was turned out of all. So it is with all unregenerate men, whatever is their outward riches and worldly enjoyments, as to spirituals they are miserably poor, very beggars indeed, (Rev. 3:17). The true riches they do not have, suitable riches for their souls they do not have, durable riches they do not have. No man is rich indeed, until he is good indeed and free indeed. God is the free man's riches, Christ is

the free man's riches, the graces of the Spirit, the privileges purchased by Christ, the promises of God, the treasures laid up in heaven, these, these are the riches of redeemed persons. But those that still remain captives and bond-slaves to Satan and to sin, have no interest in them, no title to them. If you that read these lines are one of them, whatever your outward plenty and abundance is, you are wr*etc*hedly poor. Men say of a poor person that he is worth nothing. But we might truly say of these persons, they are worth nothing, no, they are worse than nothing.

3. *Captives are not governed by the same law as freemen are.* Laws are made in favor for free subjects, but laws for slaves and bondmen are more severe, and to make their yoke heavier. Souls in spiritual bondage and captivity are not governed by the law of God which is *holy, just,* and *good,* made in favor of, and for the good of the Lord's redeemed ones, but by the laws of sin and lust, which are *unjust, oppressing,* and *tyrannical,* and oftentimes contrary to one another, *covetousness* imposing one thing on the sinner, and *prodigality* quite the contrary. The Lord's spiritual freemen are under the laws of God, but the devil's captives are under the law of sin.

4. *Captives and bondmen are put to base employment.* To toil and drudge, to dig in the mine, to work at the oar, very great and hard burdens are imposed on them. So it was with Israel in the house of bondage: the taskmasters of Egypt denied them straw, and yet required the full number of bricks, and so laid hard service on them. But there is no work so vile and sordid and base as works of sin. And yet it is the whole and only employment of spiritual bond-slaves to please the flesh and devil, and gratify their filthy lusts. What is baser slavery than to lead a sensual flesh-pleasing life? What is more sordid

drudgery than to be a servant of Satan and sin? Than to be under the commanding power of their own vile affections? To take pains to dishonor God that made them? To work and labor to undo themselves, and damn and ruin their own immortal souls? Where the work and employment of those that are redeemed from their spiritual captivity is the most *noble, rational, high*, and *honorable*, the most *delightful* and *profitable* as any can be engaged in on this side of the everlasting, full, and perfect state of the saints in glory. Such as is our *loving of God, conversing with the blessed glorious God, believing on Christ, applying of promises, living by faith, hoping, looking, longing for heaven, waiting for the glory that shall be revealed, and for the glorious appearing of our desired and longed for Lord and Savior, in getting assurance of his love, and solacing and delighting our souls with the comfort thereof when we have obtained it in using utmost diligence to escape the damnation of hell, and the everlasting torments to be endured by the devil's captives in the other endless world, and getting safe to heaven when we die in pleasing God while we live.* No, the most displeasing works to flesh and blood, are most delightful and sweet to any saint, than all the pleasures of sin, as in *mourning for sin, weeping bitterly for sin, mortifying of sin, praying against sin, watching against sin, combating and confiding with sin, warring with Satan.* Yes, the very duty of self-denial, most ungrateful to flesh and blood, has sweetness in it, and brings in that peace of conscience which surpasses the choicest delights of the devil's bond-slaves.

  5. *Captives and bond-slaves meet with hard usage in their hard work and base employment.* They are many times fed with bread and water, and that in small allowance too, are whipped and beaten when they have put forth their strength to

do their utmost. They have stripes and blows instead of a reward for what they do. Thus Israel in Egyptian bondage was beaten, when forced to gather stubble instead of straw, and could not bring in the full tally of bricks, (Exod. 5:14-16). So the devil's captives that lay themselves outmost in the devil's service shall have their wages, but what? Plagues and punishments here and hereafter, lashes, stripes, and wounds. And *that,*

1. *Sometimes from God in this world,* they have punishments and judgments inflicted on them by a just and righteous, angry God, who scourges them often in this life for their sin, and plagues them for their iniquity. So those that are slaves to their lusts are punished with filthy diseases in their bodies. "He goes after her (*a whorish woman*) straightway as an ox goes to the slaughter, or as a fool to the correction of the stocks. until a dart strikes through his liver, as a bird hastens to the snare, and does not know that it is for his life. She has cast down many wounded, yes, many strong men have been slain by her. Her house is the way to hell, going down to the chambers of death," (Prov. 7:22-27). And this you may too often see and observe in the weekly bills of mortality, that these silly filthy slaves of lust are rewarded with the loss of life. So those that are slaves to their sensitive appetite, and given to please their flesh in excessive eating and drinking are brought to poverty, (Prov. 23:21), and to death, digging their graves with their own teeth. And if they do escape outward judgments on body and estate, yet they are under spiritual judgments in their souls, as blindness of mind, hardness of heart, loss of God's favor, under the reigning power of sin, which are a thousand times worse than any bodily plagues, though less lamented.

2. *Sometimes they have lashes from their own consciences*, being filled with inward gripes and pangs, with horror and amazement, which they are not able to bear, but cry out and roar that they would rather die than live to feel these inward scourgings of their own consciences. Those two slaves of sin, and captives of the devil, Cain and Judas, when they had done the devils drudgery, the one in the murdering of his brother, the other in felling and betraying of his Lord, were so filled with inward terrors of soul that the one cries out, "My punishment is greater than I can bear," (Gen. 4:13), and would rather be slain by any that should meet him, than live to feel the terrors of his conscience. The other in the anguish of his heart confessed, "I have sinned in betraying innocent blood," and would rather hang himself and die by his own hands, and be his own executioner, than suffer what he felt in the accusations of his conscience, (Matt. 27:3-5). So these wretched slaves of Satan and sin are sometimes filled with hellish sorrows before they come to hell. Are these then not hard wages for the works of sin?

3. At the last these captives shall *certainly and eternally after death have harder wages and greater misery than any in this life*, from God, from devils, and their own consciences.

1. *God shall pour out his wrath on them*. He shall support them in their beings by his power, that they may not die under his heavy hand, and shall plague and punish them by his justice, with one hand he shall keep them from sinking into nothing, and with the other he shall inflict such wrath on them that they would rather die than live to suffer and endure.

2. *The devil shall be the executioner of God's wrath*. He that tempts them now shall torment them then. He that sets them now at work shall hereafter pay them their wages. The

very company of the devils shall scare them, and the presence of so many devils shall be no little torment to them.

3. *Their own consciences, when they come to hell shall forever vex and gnaw on them.* If now your conscience is asleep, and mercies do not waken it, and judgments do not waken it, and ministers cannot waken it, but you sin, and conscience is silent, you sin, and your friends reprove you, and ministers reprove you, but your conscience does not reprove you. Though nothing awakens your conscience now, yet the *flames of hell shall certainly awaken it*, the pains and torments there *shall certainly awaken it*. Then conscience shall be at rest no longer, and suffer you to be at rest and peace no longer, *then this sleeping lion shall awake,* and it will cry out and roar most hideously, and then you cannot go to your bouts, to bowls and sports, and recreations, that you may not hear the clamors and the outcries of your conscience. And should you say to your conscience, *Peace, be still, and let me alone*, say no more to me now, than you did when I was on the earth. What! Shall conscience say, be at peace? O *I cannot, I cannot*, though I would, yet now I cannot. God is angry, I *see* his anger, I *feel* his anger, and the smarting pain of his indignation. *I cannot be at peace.* I was blinded, but now I see, I was afraid, but now I feel, I feel such heavy strokes of revenging justice, that I *must* cry out against you for your folly, and your madness, to be a servant to your lusts, and flesh, and devil, that brought you to this place of torment. *God is lost, and Christ is lost, and heaven is lost forever,* be silent now! I cannot, O I cannot. These are intolerable pains. This fire *burns*, it burns. O it *burns*. These flames are *hot, exceedingly hot*, and you are tumbling in a lake of brimstone, and can I be silent in the midst of flames, in a burning fiery furnace, *I cannot. I must not, I will not be silent.*

Do not entreat me, for I cannot now be silent. But that which yet still is worse than all the rest, all this misery is *eternal, eternal,* woe and alas, it is *eternal.* Had this fire been to burn only for a thousand thousand years, and this pain to be endured only for a million years, yet I must have made my complaint against you, and accuse you of your madness and folly, that would serve *these devils,* against the counsels and commands of God himself. That you should be such a very fool to buy short and fading pleasures, at so dear a rate as to suffer for them such lasting pains. But when I do consider that these torments are not for certain years, but for eternity, here I am in flames, in restless, scorching flames, and which is worse, here I must forever be, *there is no end, there is no end.* Woe is me, *there is no end.* If I weep, my tears cannot quench these flames, do not put out this fire, they are but like the water which the blacksmith casts on his fire, that makes it burn so much the more. I weep but the fire burns. O let me call to all this damned crew, to all this cursed company of damned captives, *weep, weep, weep* abundantly, come and try, you would not weep out your sins, come and let us try if we can weep out these flames. Weep! So we do, so we have these thousand years, and yet our tears do not put out these flames. O then *there is no hope, there is no hope.* O to think that there is no hope, says the conscience, makes me to cry out for your folly and your madness, that would be a servant and a slave to the devil and your flesh, for which now you are tormented in these flames. You drank hard to come to this place, you swore hard to come to these torments! O how did you labor to undo yourself? How you did daily work in the service of the devil and your lusts! And you are thus rewarded for your pains. Now you feel what ministers did often tell you. Now you find what God did declare, that the wages of sin is death. Sin was your work, and hell is your wages. This, this is the fruit of your doings. This is the place of misery which the devil and your sin has led you captive to. And while you and I live (says conscience) I must be putting you in remembrance, that your sin, and your own doings have brought you to this place. So you see what hard wages these captives will receive for all the service (as they remain the devil's bond-slaves here) remaining captives to him.

     6. *Captives and bond-slaves do not have the privileges and the immunities of right that belong to free men.* Many, great, and precious are the privileges of Gods' redeemed people, purchased by the blood of Christ, but those that are yet in spiritual bondage, servants of sin, are not partakers of them. If God ever gives spiritual privileges, pardon of sin, peace with God, well-grounded peace of conscience, he will make you free, and bring you out of the house of bondage, before he puts you into the possession of Canaan. Free citizens have some advantages that those who are not free do not have, which if they would enjoy they must buy their freedom. Spiritual freedom is purchased indeed by Christ, but freely bestowed on those that are made free, and then, and not until then, are the privileges of redeemed persons conferred on them.

     7. *Captives and bond-slaves cannot satisfy the greedy desires of their cruel exactors.* Though they work hard, and toil much, yet they never think they do enough, but are ready to impose double tasks on them. When the children of Israel in Egyptian bondage had their task much increased, and complained to Pharaoh, he replied, "You are idle, you are idle, go therefore now and work," (Exod. 5:17-18). Spiritual captives in their bondage take much pains in the service of Satan and sin, yet these taskmasters never think that they sin enough, or

that they do dishonor God enough, though they sin with greediness, yet the devil would have them to be more vile still, and to be more wicked still, to swear more, and to hate God and his people, and his ways yet more. It is true, the redeemed of the Lord never do so much but they ought still to do more, to love God *more and more*, and to delight in God, and desire God still *more and more*. But the difference is great: their work is good, and the more the better, but the works of the devil's bondmen are evil, and the more the worse. And this hellish imposer will not be satisfied with all the wickedness you commit, but will provoke you still, and tempt you still, that you may sink lower, and be plagued more in hellish torments in the life to come.

8. *Captives and bond-slaves are fettered and bound in chains at the pleasure of those whose captives they are.* When Nebuchadnezzar King of Babylon "took Zedekiah King of Judah, he bound him in chains, and put him in prison until the day of his death," (Jer. 52:11). When the Philistines took Samson captive, they bound him with fetters of brass, (Judg. 16:21). So Simon Magus was bound with the bond of iniquity, (Acts 8:23). There are the "bonds and cords of duty," the commands of God, but they break these and snap asunder with ease, (Psa. 2:3), as Samson did the vines and ropes with which he was bound. But there are the "cords of sin" with which they are fast bound. "His own iniquities shall take the wicked himself, and he shall be held fast with the cords of his sin," (Prov. 5:22).

CHAPTER 3:
THE FIRST LINK – IGNORANCE

Containing ten several chains, or several links of the same chain, with which the captives and bond-slaves of Satan are bound.

Of the first. 1. *The captives and bond-slaves of Satan are bound with the chain of ignorance.* As the Syrians were smitten with blindness thought they were going after their leader to Dothan, but he brought them into the midst of their enemies, (2 Kings 6:18-20). You may lead a blind man which way you will. These captives are blind, and unless God opens their eyes they will not see their misery until they are in the midst of hell. They think they are going to heaven while they live, but after death, when the eyes of their bodies are shut, the eyes of their souls shall be opened, and behold they see themselves in the midst of hell, among devils and damned spirits. When the King of Babylon took Zedekiah captive he put out his eyes, (Jer. 52:11), and when the Philistines did take Samson captive they put out his eyes, (Judg. 16:21). And when Satan set on our first parents, and overcame them, their eyes were put out, I mean, of their understanding, they lost their knowledge of God, and of the way to eternal happiness. And all his children to this day are "born spiritually blind," and have their "understanding darkened, being alienated from the life of God, through the ignorance that is in them, because of the blindness of the heart," (Eph. 4:18). "In whom the god of this world has blinded the minds of them that do not believe, lest the light of the glorious gospel of Christ, who is the image of God, should shine into them," (2 Cor. 4:4). And this is one of the first chains which God knocks off, when he comes to set a poor captive at liberty, (Acts 26:18). But this chain or cord with which they are bound is fourfold, and so not easily broken, no, not at all but by Almighty power.

1. These captives are bound with the chain of *ignorance of sin*. The devil keeps from the eyes of his bond-slaves the evil of sin, that they should not see it in its own nature, in its proper deformity and evil shape. For sin is such a monster, that if men did see it as it is, they would abhor it, for evil *as* evil is not desirable. But Satan sets it out in the paint and dress of pleasure or profit, and so sinners are the faster held by it. It was in this way he brought mankind into bondage, and took them captive at the first, (Gen. 3:4-6), and by this means he keeps them still in slavery and captivity.

2. They are bound with the chain of *ignorance of their misery and danger by reason of sin*. These captivated souls are in danger of God's eternal wrath and curse, and do not fear it, because they do not see it. In danger of eternal torments and do not tremble at it, because it is hid from their eyes. They do not see the evil in sin, and do not consider the evil *after* sin, but think themselves to be safe, though there is but a single thread of a frail life between them and the miseries of the damned. When sinners' eyes are opened to discern their dangerous condition, the conscience awakened, they cry out, as they said, "Men and brothers, what shall we do?" (Acts 2:37). I see I am lost, tell me, O tell me, what shall I do? I am in danger of the torments of the damned, if you can, for God's sake tell me, if you have any love or pity to a poor perishing soul, tell me, what shall I do? If you know of any way or means for me to escape that hell I have deserved, tell me. Is there pardon for such sins as mine? Is there any hope for such a sinner as I have been, and as yet I am? My time is short, my days are few, and I now do see I am as near to hell as to the grave. O what shall I do that I may escape

Chapter 3: Ignorance

so great a damnation! said the jailer, (Acts 16:30-31). But while sinners are ignorant of their misery and danger Satan has them fast bound.

3. They are bound with the chain of *ignorance of the remedy to escape the misery and danger that their souls are in*. Christ is the only Savior of lost sinners, (Acts 4:12). Ignorance of Christ is a strong bond to hold men in their state of bondage. Some are *grossly* ignorant of Christ. They do not know who he was, nor what he did, nor what he did endure, ignorant of his natures, and ignorant of his offices, ignorant of his satisfaction, and of his intercession. How should these get out of bondage that cannot (while thus ignorant) believe on him that is the only redeemer of such captives? And how should they believe on him whom they have no knowledge of? Others might have some *notional* knowledge of Christ the only Redeemer, that they may be able to talk of Christ, and of his sufferings, and of his undertakings for sinners, that yet do not have any saving knowledge of him, that do not experimentally know the power of his death, and the power of his resurrection. As one might have some knowledge by hearsay of a man, that they have no acquaintance with, but are utter strangers to. If you see your sin, and if you see your misery by sin, yet if you do not see the Redeemer, have no knowledge of him, you are still captive, and fast bound in the devil's fetters.

4. They are bound in the chains of *ignorance of the covenant of grace, that was framed on purpose for the relief of captive sinners*. They do not know the terms and conditions of the new covenant, how Christ and his benefits purchased by his death are to be applied and conveyed over to them. Faith in Christ is a riddle to them, and while they remain ignorant of the way, means, and conditions proposed in the gospel, how

they should be partakers of redemption purchased by Christ, they will remain in a state of bondage and captivity. For the breaking of this cord consider (1) the necessity of spiritual knowledge without which there is no salvation, (Isa. 27:11; 2 Thess. 1:7-8). (2) The excellency of it, (Phil. 3:7-8). (3) The utility of it: it is profitable to your avoiding of sin, resisting temptation, performance of duty, escaping of misery and obtaining of glory.

The means to get it. 1. Read the Scripture. 2. Learn some catechism such as Westminster's. What, do you make children of us? You are being so ignorant; old in years, but children in point of understanding. If you were a hundred years old, if you do not know them it is no shame to learn them. 3. Set yourself under the constant preaching of the word, for there God often opens the eyes of the blind. 4. Keep company with the people of God: they will be discoursing with you of things needful for salvation. *The lips of the righteous feed many.* 5. Pray to God to open your eyes, that you may see such things as you never saw, (Matt. 20:30-33).

CHAPTER 4:
THE SECOND LINK – PREJUDICE

The Second Chain is Prejudice.

2. The captives and bond-slaves of Satan are bound *with the chain of prejudice against the ways of God and serious religion.* They have misapprehensions of godliness, hard thoughts of God, of the people of God, *they judge before they try.* And *prejudice* against a man's person makes men not hearken to his counsel, or have anything to do with him. "I knew that you were an hard, austere man, and therefore, I hid your talent in a napkin, there is what is yours," said the prejudices, slothful servant, (Matt. 25:24). *Prejudice* against a calling, a particular trade, or way and manner of living, keeps a person from being of that calling, or entering into that way. *Prejudice against the way of godliness holds sinners fast in the way of wickedness.* Slaves in Turkey have good thoughts of the condition of those that are free and at liberty in their own country, and therefore are exceedingly desirous to be in their capacity. But the slaves of Satan have a prejudiced opinion of the condition of God's freemen, and therefore do not care to be of their number. And there are several links in this chain, which we will bring forth and show you they may be broken, that poor sinners might not be any longer bound or detained in their slavery by it.

1. They have *this* prejudice against the ways of God, *that they are melancholy ways.* If they become serious in religion they must be mourning and sorrowing, and leave their pleasures, and never have a merry day more. This is a clear mistake, a groundless prejudice, for first *though there must be sorrow and mourning and repenting, yet this must come before in order to rejoicing.* Have you not sinned? And if you have

sinned, must you not, should you not sorrow? Is it not reasonable that you should grieve that you have dishonored God, provoked God, wronged and undone your own souls? If your child has rebelled against you, would you have him go on in his rebellion and disobedience still, because if he returns to his duty and is received into your favor, he should be humbled, and profess his sorrow and repentance that he ever rebelled against you? Do you expect this from your stubborn and disobedient child, and might not God expect this much more from you? And would you look on it as an aggravation of his disobedience to go on therein without sorrow and repentance, and that it would be much better for him to sorrow and return? If you would judge impartially, you would determine the case to be as reasonable between you and God.

2. *Is it not better to go mourning and repenting to heaven, than to go merrily and rejoicing to hell?* Had you not better mourn and have a sad and heavy heart for sin on earth, and hereafter be filled with the joys of heaven, than to have a light heart on earth under the heavy weight and load of sin, and be filled hereafter with the sorrows of hell? Had you not better have short sorrows for a time, and afterwards eternal joys, than to have short joys for a time, and afterwards eternal sadness and sorrows? You *have* sinned, and you *must* sorrow, on earth or in hell, here among men, or hereafter among devils, and the cursed crew of damned souls. *If you can avoid all sorrow after sin*, do you think you can have as merry and as light a heart in hell, and can lead as jolly, jovial, pleasant life in the midst of scorching fiery flames, as now you do in the ways of sin, go on and take your course. But if you cannot, as indeed you cannot, and if you could speak with a damned soul that was of your acquaintance that has been in *hell but a month or two*, he would tell you that

Chapter 4: Prejudice

you cannot. He would tell you, among us damned wr*etc*hes, there is no singing and carousing. Among us, there are no merry meetings, no parties and delights, no sports and pleasures, all full of sadness and sorrow, all lamenting their woeful case, all bewailing their miserable condition, one crying out, "Woe is me, I am undone!" And another, in another place, lamenting, "Woe is me, I am undone, woe is me, I am undone!" My sports are spent, my pleasures all past and gone, but my pain remains. My joys are gone, are fled away, but my sorrow fills my heart. Those that mourned on earth are now rejoicing in heaven. But I that had my sensual joy, my fleshly delights am sorrowing here in hell, and everything I think on, does much increase and add to my sorrow, if I think that God is lost (that I cannot get him), the glorious, gracious, blessed God is lost, this does increase my sorrow, and the heaviness of my heart. If I think that I *had time*, but it is past, *I had means of grace, ministers* once preaching to me in the name of God, forewarning me of this place, directing me, how I might have escaped these tormenting flames, and got safely to the place of bliss, and rest, and joy, and did entreat me and beseech me with that earnest seriousness, as if they could not have been happy without my salvation, as if their comfort had wrapped up in my salvation, but *these have done with me forever*. I cannot expect one sermon more, one offer of Christ, one tender of mercy more forever, many a one I had, but *now not one, not one*, woe and alas that I was ever born, not one more forever. Woe and alas, that I ever had any, and did slight them all, and because I must have not one tender experience of a Savior more forever. *This,* all *this* does add to my sorrow. Or if I think, how unwilling I was to sorrow on earth, to have my heart made heavy for my sin, nothing would please me but my pleasure. I was for mirth and joy, but the more I had of joy while I lived on the earth, the more I have of sadness and sorrow now that I am in hell. I had indeed a *short and merry life* on the earth, but now I have a long and heavy sorrowful life in the flames of hell. On earth I was for joy and no sorrow, and now in hell I have sorrow, and no joy. O I had better, I had better, I had a thousand times better repented on earth, and have been now rejoicing in heaven, than to rejoice, like a fool as I was, on earth, and must now weep and howl, and fruitlessly lament in hell. These would be the tidings of a damned soul, and far more sad and heavy than these. He would tell you, that if one goes through hell, there is not one merry heart among them all. Think then of this and see, and judge if there is any reason that you should be prejudiced against the condition of God's freemen, or the ways of holiness, because of sorrow and repentance there must be for sin. O that after this, poor captive, you may be no longer bound with this chain of the devil. But yet to knock off this fetter, and to cut this chain asunder, let us strike the other blow. Therefore, I *say*,

3. *The ways of God and holiness are not heavy, sad and melancholy ways.* Holiness is the foundation of joy, and the reason of it. Did Adam ever have a more joyful, comfortable life than when he was perfectly holy? And who are more joyful and more glad, and filled more with pleasure and delight than the saints above that are perfectly holy? And there are no persons on earth that have more cause of joy and true delight than those that are truly, though imperfectly holy. *Who* has more reason to rejoice than those that have made their peace with God, that do enjoy his favor and his gracious presence? *Who* has cause to lead a more cheerful, comfortable life, than those that have the pardon of their sin, that are the children of the ever living God? *Who* has more reason to spend their days and pilgrimage on

Chapter 4: Prejudice

earth with joy and gladness than those that are past the danger of damnation, and have the assurance, or a lively hope of being happy in the full and perfect enjoyment of the blessed God in heaven forever? Do but bring forth the grounds and reasons of your rejoicing, and set them over against the reasons of the righteous man's joy. And then judge which of the two are more weighty and more rational. Do you lead a merry life because you enjoy the world? And might not a godly man much more that enjoys God himself? Are you so pleasant in this life, because you have this world's delights? And might not a godly man much more that has heavenly delights? *I think* the thoughts of what you want should dash all the joy you take in what you have. You have riches, but you lack grace. You have the favor of your friends, but you do not have the favor of the eternal God. You have no debts to pay, or none but what you can discharge, but you do not have the pardon of your sin. This debt remains uncrossed in the book of God, and you are never able to discharge this debt. *I think* the thoughts and fears of what you shall feel hereafter should dampen your joy, and in your greatest merry mood should check your folly and change your countenance, and fill your heart with sorrow and sadness. What! You are merry when you are so near to hell? What! on the very brink and border of the bottomless pit? What! When you may not be out of hell a year or two, no, not a month or two, no, not a day or two! No, when it is more than you can tell, whether you shall be out of hell an hour or two? *Is this* the man that is so merry? *Is this* the man that pleads so much for pleasure and delight? *Is this the man indeed* that would spend his present time in joy and gladness? If this man should die today, how soon would his tune be altered? How soon, alas, how soon would his tune be changed?

What do you think you that hear me today, that know and understand the dreadful danger of a graceless, Christless, unconverted sinner? Can you see him sporting with delight about the brink of hell, and not fear and tremble, lest you see him falling down into it? Can you see him so jocund, when so near the place of utter darkness, and not stand amazed at his boldness and his blindness? Do not your hearts pity such a one, though he has no pity for himself? Come sinner, judge yourself, if of all men in the world you have any cause of such a joyful life that you plead for. And whether if you would lead a cheerful life indeed, it would not be your *wiser, surer, safer* course to leave your serving of the devil and your lusts, and to break your cords and chains by which you have been bound, and held captive for so many years as you have been.

Besides, what are these pleasures which you find in the creature? What are these joys and comforts which you fetch from anything besides God, or below God? Are they not sensual and brutish? Are they not only found in the sensitive part of your soul, and not in the more noble and rational part? Do you place your pleasure and delights in eating and drinking, and gratifying your sensitive appetite? Why your very beast, your horse, your dog has this delight as well as you! And some creatures have this delight more than man. I can tell you of a man that has tried more than what these pleasures are, that had a greater estate, and greater varieties of all sorts to delight himself, that has made such search what there is in all things under the sun to delight the heart of man, that no man that comes after him can do more. And yet he has left it on record from his own experience, "that all is vanity and vexation of spirit," and that is Solomon, (Eccl. 2). Take your book and read it. His conclusion is that the delights and pleasures fetched from things above the sun do far surpass and exceed all pleasures and delight taken from all things under the sun. The same man that tells you that all under the sun is vanity, does also tell you that the ways of wisdom, "are ways of pleasantness, and all her paths are peace," (Prov. 3:17).

Come then, poor captive sinners, *come and try* what comforts and delights are to be found in the ways and service of our God, do not judge before you try. How can *you* tell, what are the ways of God, before you have experienced what they are? How can *you* tell, there are no comforts, joys that the saints met with, when you were never qualified for those comforts and those joys? I do not persuade you to cast away a comfortable life, but to change it for a better life. I do not persuade you to leave delights and pleasures, but to change them for more *noble*, more *rational*, more *spiritual*, more *durable* delights. Come and get a real taste and relish of the sweet delights in *communion with God, in the sense of his love, in a right applying of his promises, in hoping for his kingdom*. And if you do not like them better, and find them sweeter, then return again to your present comforts, and fetch them again from the same objects that you do now. But then be sure your heart is changed, that you might taste indeed the sweetness of delights and comforts in God, in Christ, in the promises and privileges of the gospel, and I dare be bold to say, you will then say these are *better, greater, sweeter* than any you ever found before in Satan's service, or in the way of sin. Come therefore, come and try.

Objection. Why do we need that? Though we have not tried ourselves, yet we see how it is by those that have? Do we not see that those that have forsaken their former ways, and since have become more precise and strict, that they spend their days in sorrow, always mourning and complaining, with tears and countenances showing the heaviness and sadness and sorrow of their hearts?

Answer. 1. *What, all! Always! It is not so!* There are those believers that are sometimes filled with unspeakable joy, (1 Peter 4:8), that are so delighted with the love of God to their souls, and with hopes of glory that they can and do rejoice in the sorest tribulation, (Rom. 5:3), that have such believing views of future glory, and such present tastes of the sweetness of gospel-privileges that fills their souls with such holy admirations, and divine comforts, that cannot be expressed with words, (1 John 3:1).

2. Those that you see mourning, weeping, and grieving much for their sins, *they have cause and ground and reason to rejoice, and so you that are yet captives to the devil do not have.* And are they not in a better condition that have ground and reason to rejoice, but do not, than you that do rejoice when you have no cause or reason to do so? Of the two I would rather have my soul in their soul's condition than in yours.

3. *You do not know how sweet and pleasant and delightful these bitter tears of repentance are to them that shed most of them.* It is exceedingly comfortable to have a heart to mourn and grieve kindly for their sins. Their tears you see, but their inward peace and comfort that often follows after these, you do not take notice of.

4. *But how do you know the true cause and reason of their sorrow?* You are apt to impute it to the way that they walk in. Did any truly godly soul that leads the saddest and most sorrowful life ever tell you that his sorrow is because *now* he has become a holy man? Did any ever tell you that it is because they have left their former wicked ways? And because they

have become new creatures, and have given up their names, their wills, their hearts, and all to God and Christ? If this, and no such like thing is the cause of their sadness, is there any reason you should be so prejudiced against the state of the Lord's redeemed ones, and please yourself rather in this present bonds, than to desire to be released and delivered from them? But what if you see them shed these tears, and the sorrow you perceive they are filled with, *is,*

    1. Because *they were captives to the devil for so long, and served sin and lust so long,* that they lay in chains and fetters so long, when a Redeemer was so often offered to them, and they did not have hearts to close with him sooner than they did, that they served the devil, a hard and cruel master so long, and came into Christ, so good and so gracious a Lord, as by experience now they find to be, and his work and wages to be so sweet, that they came to him so late. If this is the true reason, is their sorrow than any real reason of your prejudice against godliness? No, truly, it does commend it so much the more.

    2. What if the reason of their sorrow is because *they have made no more progress in holiness since they came into the ways of holiness?* That they have attained no more likeness to God, to no more faith and love, to no more humility and heavenly-mindedness. They are weeping and mourning as *you see,* not because they are come into the ways of God, *as you do think,* but because they have not yet gone further in them. Not because they have left their sin, but because they sinned so much, and now can leave their sin no more. They are so sorrowful because they are no more fruitful, because they are no better. Ask them if this is not the reason, and if so, is there any reason their sorrow should prejudice your hearts against godliness? No, truly, it does commend it so much the more,

when they that have a true and real taste of the sweetness of it, sorrow so much because they have attained to no more degrees of it.

3. What if the reason of their sorrow is because *they can do no more for God and Christ by way of thankfulness to him who has done so much for them as of bond-slaves to make them free?* That God should give his own only Son, and Christ should give himself, his life, his soul, his blood for a ransom to bring them out of their captivity, to deliver them from hell and wrath to come and make them that were *the other day* in bondage, and liable to damnation, *now* meet to be partakers in the inheritance of the saints in light. And yet that they can honor him no more might be the reason of their sorrow.

4. What if the reason of their sorrow is because *they see so many still remain in bonds,* so many still continue servants to the devil, and to sin, and do refuse to serve and live toward the blessed, holy, glorious God? And is this matter of sorrow not indeed to see the devil leading precious and immortal souls captive to hell? That men should be so forward to follow the devil, their *destroyer* to eternal torments, and so backward to follow Christ, the only *Savior* to eternal joys? These are mourning, not because they are made free, but because you and so many more remain captives to the devil.

5. *What if the reason of their sorrow is for their sin which they committed when they were bond-slaves to the devil.* Does this discommend holiness, to bewail wickedness, or is this for the credit and commendation of your sinful way of life, that men that are serious and have their eyes opened, do see so much evil in it, that they think they can never lament it enough? Certainly it does disgrace the way of sin.

2. Another link in this chain of prejudice by which these captives are bound is *the offence they take from the inward mean condition of God's redeemed people*. They see them to be the poorer sort of people that are full of zeal for the strictness in religion. The rich men, and the great men, and the *gallants* are not of this way. This purchased and proclaimed and bestowed liberty on poor captive sinners. "Is this not the carpenter's son? They were offended at him," (Matt. 13:55, 57). And the Pharisees were held in this bond. "No man ever spoke like this man. Then answered the Pharisees, Are you also deceived? Have any of the rulers or the Pharisees believed on him? But this people who do not know the law are cursed," (John 7:46-49). Let us try to remove this prejudice, and break this bond in these five answers briefly.

1. *Shall the greatness and the riches, and the gallantry of sinners advantage them anything beyond the grace, or profit them one bit in another world, or at the bar of God?* Shall they be preserved from hell, and the torments of the damned because they are rich and great, and prosper in the world? Or shall they be saved or received into heaven when they die, because they were rich while they lived in the world? Will not death strip them of their estates, of their costly robes? Will not death make these *gallants* as *ghastly* as the poor, and is there any difference between the corps of the *nicest dame, and the poorest beggar?* Must not the one rot in the earth as well as the other? And be fed on by worms? Or will the very worms make any difference between the one and the other? When the graves are opened, where the *poor and rich* were buried, and rotten, and their *skulls and bones* are cast up, can you know the bones and skulls of the rich from the bones and skulls of the poor? Or which it was that was clothed with silks, and which with rags

or coarser cloth? Which it was that was fed with sweetest morsels, and with greatest delicacies, and which with harder fare and meaner diet? No, you cannot. Why then, when you shall be so soon equalized with the poorest beggar, are you so prejudiced by the meanness of Christ's followers? *Must you not* stand as naked before the just tribunal of an impartial God as those that now for their poverty you condemn and scorn? Or shall *you* appear in your *locks and curls*, with which you so much vainly pride yourselves? Shall you appear with your rings, and jewels, and bracelets, or be then regarded, because you trick up your mortal bodies with such things now? No, no, it is more likely you will then wish you had never had them, you had never used them, especially since your heart was so puffed up with pride, that you disdained redemption by Christ, because many of his followers were so far below you in outward enjoyments of the world.

2. *What if the rich and poor were sick of the same disease, and there was but only one remedy for the recovering of both, would the rich refuse the only remedy, because the poorer sort do make use of it?* Would they rather die, and go to their graves, or lie in pain rather than use the same remedy that the meaner sort are cured by? This is the very case, a prince and a beggar, the noble and the ignoble, high and low, rich and poor are sick of the same soul-distempers, *all are all alike* guilty of and polluted with original sin, all are by nature children of wrath, under the curse of the law, have deserved the damnation of hell. And there is but *only one way* of salvation, only one Redeemer and Savior, (Acts 4:12). And the way and means to be partakers of Christ and his benefits is *one and the same to all*. God has not prescribed *one* way of salvation to the rich, and *another* to the poor, but the *same* to both. Must the poor

believe, so must the rich, or be damned. Must the poor be holy and converted, so must the rich, or else never see God, nor enter into his kingdom. Will you then rather perish forever, than be saved the same way, and by the same means that the poorer sort are saved by? If you are so stout and proud, and high-minded, for this reason to neglect God, *let him alone*, and for this reason to reject Christ, *let him alone*, and in the end see who will have cause to complain, God or you, and who will have the worst of it, the poor or you.

3. *If it is the pleasure of God, to call and convert the meaner sort of people, to bestow his Son, his Spirit, and his grace on them, what right do you have to quarrel with God, or be offended at the method of his grace?* Is not Christ God's own gift, and his grace and kingdom, and eternal life his own gift, and in his own power, and may he not give it to whom he wills? What if God has chosen the poor in this world to make them rich in faith, and to be heirs of glory, (James 2:5). Will you rather remain children of wrath, and captives still to sin and Satan, than to be *co-heirs with such* contemptibility in your eyes? Who do you think will be the losers and the sufferers but yourselves? If their poverty and low estate does not diminish God's love to them, there is no reason it should cause or increase your prejudice against the only way to eternal happiness.

4. *It is better to be a poor man, and to be a freeman than to be a rich man under close restraint and bondage.* Civil liberty is to be preferred before many enjoyments, much more is spiritual freedom to be valued and desired above honors, pleasures, and profits of the world. Is it not better to be in a low condition while you live and be saved when you die, than to be ungodly, though rich in this world, and damned in the next? Is

it not better to go with truly gracious and believing persons (though poor) to heaven and eternal glory, than with Christless, graceless persons (though rich and honorable) to everlasting torments?

5. *If you speak of the true riches, and who are rich indeed, believers are not poor.* Then the scale is turned, then the ungodly are the poor, and the godly are the rich. These have the *surest* riches, the *safest*, the most *suitable* and the most *lasting*, the *everlasting* riches. God is their riches, and Christ in who are unsearchable riches, is their riches. And the treasures that are above are their riches. They are *rich in grace*, and *rich in promises*, and *rich in special spiritual privileges*. And when worldly riches shall fail, and stand you in no stead, they will not profit, nor advantage you. Then their riches shall comfort them and remain with them and be continued to them forever. And is there now any reason why you should be bound with this bond of prejudice against the freedom you might have by Christ, because many whom Christ makes free are poor and mean in their outward condition in the world?

3. Another link in this chain of prejudice by which these captives are bound is *that the way by which spiritual freedom is obtained is a persecuted way, it is full of thorny troubles and of smarting tribulations.* Such as Christ frees, they are many times afflicted with the loss of goods, with the loss of outward liberty, and of life itself. Such are mocked, scorned, and reproached, and do often suffer while others flourish and prosper. This indeed has been a strong temptation to good and gracious men, as to David (Psa. 73), and to Jeremiah (Jer. 12:1), and to Habakkuk (Hab. 1:13-14). But it is a strong bond by which wicked men are held back from entering into the way in which they might be made free. But O, that God would enable

you to break this bond, and cut in two this chain, by working on your hearts such considerations as these following.

1. *They have peace with God when they have trouble in the world.* They have favor with God when they have frowns from men. When men are their foes, God is their friend. Though men loathe them, yet God loves them. Though men are against them, and devils are against them, yet God is for them. Yes, all in God is for them. His mercy is for them, his power is for them, his truth is for them. And is there not more in peace and friendship with God to make them happy than in all the troubles they have from men to make them miserable? And is it not better to have one powerful, true, eternal God to be one's friend, though all the world should be one's enemy, than to have such a God to be one's enemy, and weak and mortal men to be one's friend. What will come of you, while in your sins you are at rest and ease, yet God is against you, his justice is against you, his truth is against you, and his power is against you. And as God's people shall find God to be the surest friend, so the wicked shall find him to be the sorest enemy.

2. *Though they have outward troubles, yet they have inward joys and comforts.* As they have peace with God, so they have peace in and with themselves. And their joy is such that no man can take it from them. Their outward enjoyments and their lives they may take from them, but they cannot take their comfort and their joy from them, (John 16:22). The testimony of their conscience makes them to rejoice, (2 Cor. 1:12). They are filled with such inward consolations that they can triumph and sing in their outward tribulations, (Rom. 5:3), when cast and bound in prison, (Acts 16:23-25), when beaten and scourged, (Acts 5:40-41), and the *sweetness of their inward comforts* does abate and take away the *bitterness of their*

outward sorrows. You see their troubles, you see their afflictions, but you are strangers to their comforts, or else you would not be so prejudiced against the way of holiness for the outward evils that befall them that walk therein.

3. *The troubles and the sufferings of God's redeemed ones are but short, but for a little, little while.* But the sufferings of the devil's captives are long and lasting, for a *long, long, long eternity.* Compare their sufferings here with the eternal joys they shall have hereafter and they are short. Or with the eternal torments that the slaves of sin shall hereafter feel, and so they are but for a moment, at their longest their sufferings shall last, no longer than their life on earth shall last, and that will be but for a while. After a few more years or months, or weeks, and all their sorrow shall be over, past and gone, and in as short a time, your joy and ease will pass away and return no more forever. Their sufferings will shortly end, and their rest and ease and joy begin, but never end, and your ease will shortly end, and your sufferings and sorrows will begin, but never, never end. What do you think now? Is it not better to be in trouble for a while, and afterwards be lodged in a place of everlasting rest, and love and joy, than to live at ease a while in sin, and afterwards roll and tumble in a restless lake of burning brimstone to all eternity. If you are not of this mind now, it will not be long before you will.

4. *The troubles of God's holy, humbly, sanctified people, they are but light as well as short.* True indeed, in themselves they may be heavy, and to flesh and blood they may be heavy, but comparatively they are but light. Compare them with that weighty crown of glory that shall be put on their heads, and so they are but light, (2 Cor. 4:17), not worthy to be compared with it, (Rom. 8:18). And compare their troubles here

with the sufferings of the devil's captives hereafter, and still they will be found to be but light. The sufferings of the one are from *angry and displeased men*, but the sufferings of the other are from *an angry and offended God.* And is the arm of men to be compared with the arm of God? The wrath of men to the wrath of God? And can feeble men lay on such blows as can a strong and mighty God? Can a child strike such a stroke as a mighty giant can? O you shall shortly feel the heavy weight of God's revenging fury. And if you think it will not be so bad, nor so heavy on you, but you shall do well enough to bear it. Tell me, why then do you cry out and roar under extremity of the toothache? Why do you complain and say, you cannot rest nor sleep? Why do you make so great a stir under a fit of colic, gout, or stone? Why do you not say, this is nothing to be born? This is easy to be endured? Why do you then so frown and fret, and make such bitter lamentation? But alas what is this to the torments of the damned? To lying in a fiery furnace? In a place of utter darkness, where there shall be weeping and wailing, and gnashing of teeth forever? Where the worm never dies, and the fire shall not be quenched? What is this to lying in those flames which God on purpose has caused to burn, for the punishment of sin? To lying in that place, which God on purpose has provided for the showing forth of the glory of his justice, and his holiness, and his utter hatred of sin, in pouring out his fury, and his sorest indignation in the punishment of the sinner. O that God would break this bond, that by it you might no longer be kept as bond-slaves to the devil.

4. Another link in this chain of prejudice, by which these captives are bound is their *apprehension of the difficulty of religious duties.* The duties to be performed, as *mortification of sin, self-denial, heavenly-mindedness, fervent prayer,*

constant, holy, watchfulness, in the whole course of life, *close and narrow self-examination,* these and such like are displeasing, because of the difficulty they apprehend in them, and will not be at the pains to perform them, and if they try, they find it to be an heavy and a grievous burden and cast it off again. Towards the breaking of this bond consider.

    1. *It is to sinful man, and the sinful part of man that holy duties are so displeasing and so burdensome.* It is because your souls are distempered, and not from anything in the nature of holiness. This is plain, because the *angels of God* that are without sin, do not find it a burden but a pleasure to be obedient unto God. And when the *people of God* shall be perfectly cured of all soul-diseases they shall not find any difficulty or tedious irksomeness in constant and perpetual holy actings. And *man* as made *at first by God,* took pleasure, and did find great delight in his conformity to the will of God. It is plainly then from the corruption of your depraved nature, and the wickedness of your own hearts, that you find this difficulty in religion, and that holiness is such a burden to you. As a man that is distempered does not favor nor relish his food; what others taste sweetness in, is bitter to him; the cause is not in the meat, but in the palate. Should this man cry out, "My meat is bitter," or rather, "my disease is great and dangerous?" Or should he therefore refuse his sustenance, and rather die with hunger than receive his food? So should you cry out and complain, "Godliness is burdensome, and religion is a tedious task?" Or rather blame the corruption of your heart, that which is pleasant and delightful to others is so heavy and displeasing to you? Do you say *God's commands are grievous,* others have said they are not so, (1 John 5:3). Do you say, *Christ's yoke is heavy,* and his burden not to be borne? Christ tells you, "His

yoke is easy, and his burden is light," (Matt. 11:30). Do *you find* the serious constant study of the holy Word of God to be burdensome to you? *David* found it to be sweet, and pleasant, and delightful, (Psa. 115:35), as sweet to him as riches to a worldly man, (Psa. 119:14), and "better to him than thousands of gold and silver," (Psa. 19:72). Do *you find* God's commands to be to you as bitter as gall? Others have found them to be sweeter than honey, or the honeycomb, (Psa. 19:10). Are they unpleasant *to you?* They are to others more desirable than their necessary food, (Job 23:12). Where does this come to pass, that the same commands of God, and the same religious duties are sweet to others, but bitter to you, pleasant to others but burdensome to you? Is it not apparent that it is from the wickedness of your own depraved hearts? And have you distempered yourselves and now cry out of the burden of the ways of God? Have you done what you ought not to do, and by it became weak and unable, and then cast the blame on the commands of God, that is indeed, on God himself? It is not your wisdom but your wickedness to do so.

2. *It is the external part of duties without the enjoyment of God in them that makes them to be so heavy and so burdensome to you,* because you do not get into the spiritual part of religious performances. To pray indeed and not to meet with God in prayer, to sit and hear, to fast and afflict the body without communion with God, this is that which is the cause of this tediousness in religion you do so much cry out against. But in the internal part of religion, in loving of God, in believing on Christ, in meeting with God, in the desires of the soul after God there is sweetness, and when it is thus with the soul, it finds not duty to be a burden. But there the soul could dwell, there it could with pleasure stay and make its abode.

No, there is more true delight in denying the pleasures of the flesh, than in fulfilling them. You have no experience of these things, but ask God's people, and they will tell you, this is so. Inquire of them and they will assure you that this is so. And should you be so prejudiced against what you do not know? If you did know, your prejudice would quickly be removed. You engage in the *matter* of a duty, and do not mind the *manner* of it, and that increases your prejudice against it. Come then, love God in prayer, mourn for sin in prayer. Were you able and subjects capable of applying promises to yourselves, promises of pardon, and promises of heaven, as your own, in reading and hearing of the word, then it would be sweet and pleasant. Though you in your unconverted state do not *find* it to be so, yet do not say, it is not so, but believe them that have had experience, and come over to God and Christ indeed, and then with the Samaritans you will say, as they to the woman, "Now we believe, not because of your saying, for we have heard him ourselves, and know that he is indeed the Christ, the Savior of the world," (John 4:42). Or you will find, as the Queen of Sheba said concerning Solomon, "She said to the king, it was a true report that I heard in my own land of your acts, and of your wisdom. Howbeit, I did not believe the words until I came and my eyes have seen it. And behold, the half was not told me. Your wisdom and prosperity exceeds the fame which I heard. Happy are your men, happy are these your servants which stand continually before you, and hear your wisdom," (1 Kings 10:4-5). The flesh makes false reports of the ways of God, but *come and try*, and you will say, you heard much was said against the tediousness of religion, and for the easiness of Christ's yoke, but now I find, the one half was not expressed, of what might be experienced of the delight and sweetness in it, which takes off the burdensomeness of it.

3. *Set the necessity of being found in the ways of God against the difficulty of walking in them.* If a thing is difficult and unpleasing, yet if you apprehend it to be necessary, that it must be done, you set on it. It is a burden to some people to take medicine, but when they are so sick that they must take it or die, they set themselves to it. Sirs, do not stand disputing, it is a difficult matter to be holy, to love God, to turn from sin, it is a burden to you to serve God. Hard or not hard, it must be done, burden or no burden, it must be done, or you die and that forever. You must do the things that God requires, repent, believe, become new creatures, receive Christ, be holy, or you must be damned. Here is no trifling in the case. Here is no arguing *pro* and *con* to be admitted, these things must be done, or your souls shall not be saved. If the word of God is true, this is true. They are not my words but the words of the true eternal God. Turn and see, read the following: "And he said unto them, Go ye into the entire world, and preach the gospel to every creature. He that believeth and is baptized shall be saved; but he that believeth not shall be damned," (Mark 16:15-16). "For if ye live after the flesh, ye shall die: but if ye through the Spirit do mortify the deeds of the body, ye shall live," (Rom. 8:13). "Jesus answered and said unto him, Verily, verily, I say unto thee, Except a man be born again, he cannot see the kingdom of God," (John 3:3). "I tell you, Nay: but, except ye repent, ye shall all likewise perish. Or those eighteen, upon whom the tower in Siloam fell, and slew them, think ye that they were sinners above all men that dwelt in Jerusalem? I tell you, Nay: but, except ye repent, ye shall all likewise perish," (Luke 13:3-5). "Be

not deceived; God is not mocked: for whatsoever a man soweth, that shall he also reap.

For he that soweth to his flesh shall of the flesh reap corruption; but he that soweth to the Spirit shall of the Spirit reap life everlasting," (Gal. 6:7-8). "Now the works of the flesh are manifest, which are these; adultery, fornication, uncleanness, lasciviousness, Idolatry, witchcraft, hatred, variance, emulations, wrath, strife, seditions, heresies, Envyings, murders, drunkenness, revellings, and such like: of the which I tell you before, as I have also told you in time past, that they which do such things shall not inherit the kingdom of God," (Gal. 5:19-21). 1 Cor. 6:9-10; Rev. 20:8. And he also said, "Verily I say unto you, Except ye be converted, and become as little children, ye shall not enter into the kingdom of heaven," (Matt. 18:3). What do you say now? Do you believe this to be the word of God or not? Do you believe you must be judged by it, be damned or saved according to this word? Does God not speak his mind plainly, and declare his purpose, and his unalterable resolution, that you must *turn to him, or burn in hell*? That you must repent and believe, and that *quickly too*, or you must be lost forever? Why do you *poor captive sinner*, stand thus delaying and loitering, crying it is hard to leave my sins, to repent, a burden to give myself to holy duties. Speak, sinner, in the name of God I demand your answer, will you do what God requires, or will you not? Is it not extremely necessary, if you will be saved? And if it is *so difficult*, and *so necessary*, why are you so long before you go about it? Had you not more need to take all the time before you to do this work that is so hard and yet so necessary. Why then do you put it off until you come to be sick, and until you come to die? Are you likely to be fit for the hardest work when you shall be fit for no work at all? Do you sometimes think that this is easy, and therefore you defer it to the last, and sometimes think it so hard for you to meddle with it at all? *Poor captive soul!* Do you so turn and wind in your own thoughts, and harbor anything that may prolong the time of your captivity, and bind you faster and faster still in your fetters and your chains? Will you still say, it is a hard case, it is a burdensome thing to be really religious, to be truly holy, then tell me further.

4. *Will it not be a harder case to bear the wrath of God forever?* Is duty now a burden to you? And will not the torments of hell be a burden to you? Can you not bear the burden of a holy life? And can you bear the damnation of hell? Do you not think, the *thoughts* of the loss of God and Christ, and heaven will be an heavy and continual burden to you? Do you not think the *fight* of devils round about you, will not be a burden to thee? And your constant *hearing* of such horrible howlings, such doleful lamentations, such bitter cries of *woe, woe,* forever *woe,* that we were born, what *shall we do, what shall we do, woe and alas what shall we do, this place is hot, is hot, O, O, it is exceedingly hot, this pain is great, this pain is great, O, it is exceedingly great, it is extreme, it is extreme.* And which is worse and does increase our woe and sorrow, it is *eternal too, it is eternal too!* Will not such hearing of such dreadful outcries be a burden to you? Do you not, *poor captive sinner,* think what you shall feel in pain on *your body,* by the burning of fiery flames, and the anguish in *your soul* by the ever-gnawings of the never-dying worm, will not be a burden to you? Is it difficult to love God, and will it not be difficult to bear the wrath of God? Is it difficult to *serve him,* and will it not be difficult to *suffer* from him? I tell you, it will be the hardest task that you were ever put on, to bear the torments of

the damned. O, *come* then, sinner, *come away*, though it is hard to leave your sins, yet do it, though it is hard to walk strictly before the Lord, yet come and do it, or else something will befall you shortly, that you shall say, is hard to suffer.

5. This difficulty that you find in religious duties is *because as yet you have no strength but what is your own to do them with*. But if you do renounce the devil and the flesh, and give yourself to God and Christ, you shall have help from heaven, and then they will be easier to you. While you are in bonds of sin, you have neither *strength* nor *skill* to do them with, and that makes it hard. But if God makes you free, you shall have both, and then it will be easy. If you want skill, God will show you, and if you want strength, God will *help* you, and then praying work, and repenting work, will go more smoothly forward. When God shall come and *break* and *melt* your heart, it will be easier to repent. When God shall come, and give to you, a *sight* and *sense* of your sins and that which you lack, of your lack of grace and pardon, of your lack of Christ and a renewed heart, it will be easier for you to bewail your sins, and to pray and beg supplies for what you want. God is not an hard master to his servants, to put them on work, and give them neither power nor reward, for he gives both to those that in sincerity give up themselves to his service. That though without Christ we can do nothing, (John 15:5), yet being strengthened by Christ, we can do all things in order to the saving of our souls, (Phil. 4:13), and the Spirit is *purchased* and *promised* by Christ, to help the weaknesses and infirmities of his servants, (Rom. 8:26). He shall help you with *words* in prayer, to express your wants, your heart, and your desires to God, and when you want words, he shall help you, with *sighs* and *sobs*, and *tears*, which are powerful pleadings with the

Chapter 4: Prejudice

Lord, who understands the stammerings and the groanings of his children, (Rom. 8:27).

So I have showed the *second chain* with which these captives are bound, the prejudice of their hearts against the holy ways of God's redeemed, and free newborn people, and have endeavored to cut it in two, to knock it off. But alas this is too hard a work for man to do, for any ministry on earth to do. Sinners are so fast locked in their fetters that it requires almighty power to break them that the captive may escape and be set at liberty. O that therefore God would come, and burst and break it quite asunder! O that God would come and take it off, were it but from one or two among you this day! That though you came captives in your chain, yet you might go home free men, and at liberty. *But yet* something is required from you, that you should consider and weigh with yourselves impartially and deliberately what has been said, to remove this prejudice of your hearts which makes you like your present captive state, and not desirous to come forth from it. And if what has been spoken is not sufficient ground to silence these carnal pleas, I beg the prayers of the congregation and even now of the readers for me, that God would forgive my weakness, and pardon my unskillfulness, that know no better how to deliver a message from the Lord, and to pray that for the future I might be more fitted for this weighty work. But if there is evidence of truth in what has been delivered and spoken in your ears, I charge you *in the name of the dreadful and eternal God, in the name of Christ my Lord that sent me,* that you do not slight it. If I have spoken my own words, fling them back in my face, and tell me that I lie, but if it is according to the Scripture, then slight them at your peril. Either show where I have erred, or else submit to it. But if you, whoever you are, or whatever name you are called by, are convinced in your conscience, and your reason and judgment is satisfied that these grounds of prejudice have been made to appear to be in vain and frivolous, and yet shall on these accounts choose rather to continue in your captive state than to come to Christ and be made free, and go to *your grave, and hell,* with these fetters on your soul, know that you are by it rendered inexcusable.

CHAPTER 5: THE THIRD LINK – LOVE OF THE WORLD

The third chain is the love of the world.

A third chain by which these captives are bound is *the immoderate and prevailing love of the profits and riches of this world.* This binds thousands fast that they will not, cannot stir or move, or come to Christ, that they may be set at liberty. These are bound with *chains of gold.* And because they are golden chains, therefore they like them so much the more. The devil does not care about cost, if by any means he can keep you still in bondage. He will not grudge you from the *riches of the world,* if he can keep you *out of heaven.* Many moral men that have escaped the gross pollutions of the world, that are no swearers, nor drunkards, nor openly profane, that bless themselves with the thoughts of their supposed good condition, yet are as sure the *devil's prisoners,* and in slavery and bondage, and shall as certainly perish and be damned (except they get this bond broken) as any drunkard in the town, or parish where they live. Believe this as a certain truth, for the mouth of the Lord has spoken it. Turn and read Ephesians 5:5. Shall the whoremonger be saved, or the world-monger? Shall the unclean person inherit the kingdom of God, or the person that has his heart and affections set on the world? And the Holy Spirit gives a reason, because such a man is *an idolater,* making his *gold* his *god.* That love and delight, and joy which God should have is given to the world, and that God will never bear. That hope and trust which should be placed in the living God is placed in uncertain riches, and this the jealous God will never brook. Turn again to Colossians 3:5-6. God tells you this over and over, in one place after another, so that you might the more beware of being kept in bondage by this golden chain, which is so very strong that the Lord does tell us, *the love of money is the root of all evil,* (1 Tim. 6:10). There are many branches of sin which shoot out in the lives of men, but all do grow on this root, the heart being fixed in its love to the world.

1. *Omissions of duty*, neglect of closet and family prayer, worldliness is the root. The heart is so eager after riches that they have no time, nor leisure for better things. And when they have time, yet the worldly heart is indisposed to perform them, and listless to heavenly employment.

2. *Commissions of sin*, the use of false balances, and deceitful measures, overreaching, breach of promises, falsifying their words, speaking often against conscience, the seller commending his goods beyond, and above what he knows them to be, affirming that they cost him more than they did, and if he does not sell them for so much, he shall be a loser by them, and all this to defraud the buyer to an higher price. And the buyer discommends the seller's ware, saying, it is nothing, it is nothing. To bring him down to a lower rate, but all this comes from this evil bitter root, the *immoderate love of the world.* Many men engage in company and are overtaken with excessive drinking, and when reproved, will reply. It was with such as were my customers, and I can avoid such occasions, if I will not drink with some, they will not trade with me, except I go to the alehouse, or the tavern, I shall lose the taking of many dollars. Shall you so? Yes, and *would prevent many drunken bouts.* But what do you have houses of your own for, and what are your shops for, and what is the exchange for, but for your trades and dealing in the world. It is a shame that it is brought into so great a custom, *that many cannot buy and sell but over*

a pot. But if you do go, what need do you have to drink to excess? Do others urge you? But they cannot, they do not *force* you, is it not your own hand that often lifts the glass to your mouth? And is not your hand commanded by your own will to do it? You had better be without such a customer, and without the profit you gain by him, than to sin, and wound, and lose your soul. But this branch of wickedness grows on this cursed root, the love of money, which if some may gain, they will go from one drinking place into another. Yes, and to hell too at the last, if they might but gain, what their heart does love so much while they are here. By this bond was Balaam bound, "who loved the wages of unrighteousness," (2 Peter 2:15). And Achan, (Josh. 7:20-21). And Gehazi, who framed falsehoods for worldly profit, and afterwards would have hid it from his master with a lie "to the end," (2 Kings 5:20). And the young man whom, when Christ saw so fast fettered with this chain, (Matt. 19:21-22), he preached to his disciples that it was exceedingly hard for a rich man to be saved. Though he explained that it is not so much the having as the over-loving of them, and trusting in them that hinders men's salvation, (Mark 10:24). Judas also was detained as the devil's captive, being bound with this bond, who for the sake of money sold his Lord, and soul and all, (Matt. 26:14-16). And Demas, (2 Tim. 4:10). And doubtless thousands are now in everlasting chains of darkness, being kept in bondage by the love of the world, while they lived in the world. But shall we try to break this bond, we shall not win them for Jesus Christ, for you cannot love God and the world too with a prevailing and predominant love, (1 John 2:15; Jas. 4:4). And while you love the world you cannot value Christ, nor are you worthy of him, (Matt. 10:37-38). *Consider,*

1. *Do you not have other things and better things to set the love of your hearts on?* And is there not a God and Christ for you to love And, (1) is not God infinitely a more noble and excellent object for your love? (2) Is he not a more suitable good to your soul? (3) Is he not a sufficient good? And, therefore (4) a satisfying good? (5) Is he not a more necessary good, seeing without the things of the world you may be happy, but not without God? (6) Is he not a more durable, lasting, everlasting good? Do but get a right knowledge of God and the world, and then you will see cause to call off your heart from earthly things, and set them on God.

2. *Should you set your heart and love on earthly things which you must shortly leave, and cannot carry with you into another world?* Do you forget that you are a pilgrim on earth, and that this is not the place of your abode? After you slept out a few more nights, and walked up and down a few more days, will not your last hour come, when you must bid *adieu* to all this world, and take your farewell of all on earth? Whether you shall go to heaven or to hell, here you must not tarry. Whether you shall be damned or saved, or go to God or devils, here you must not abide. And will you take your riches with you? See that silver and gold do not go in another world. Whether you go to heaven or to hell after death, riches will be of no use to you. God would then stand by you, and Christ would then stand by you, and grace would then go with you, but you must leave your worldly riches, and they will then leave you, when you stand in the greatest need of comfort and support, (Luke 12:19-20; Psa. 49:17; Eccl. 5:15; 1 Tim. 6:7). Why will you then so fix your heart on these things, and be fettered and entangled with the love of them and by it to be kept from God, and Christ, and heaven forever.

3. *Can these things comfort you at your departure?* Or will it not be then that your soul has loved the world, but not God and Christ? Did you never stand by the bedside of a dying man, who in the anguish of his soul has roared and cried out, *Woe is me, that I have spent my time in laboring for the world, for this vain and empty world, while God and Christ and heaven have been neglected by me! Of if I had loved God and Christ as I have loved the world, I would now be a happy, blessed man. Though I am a dying man, yet I would now be a happy blessed man. God would now have comforted me, and Christ would now have comforted me, and solid lively hopes of heaven would now have comforted me, but the things that had my heart, and all my love, they do not comfort, I find, I feel they do not comfort me.* Shall you neither stay to enjoy them here, and can you not take them with you where you are going, nor yet will they comfort you in your passage to eternity, and is it reasonable then that you should be in this way fettered and bound in your love to them, as to keep you from God and Christ, here and hereafter too?

4. *Was this the end for which you were born, and did God give you such affections as love desire and delight, that you should set them on such things as these?* Did God make these things to be the chief object of your soul's affections for these things? Did God send you into this world to scrape together a heap of *refined earth*, and then to love it when you have done, better than himself that made you? Is not this a setting of God below the creature, and exalting the creature in the room of God? Is not this to lose the end of your creation?

5. *Is not this to love such things as do not, cannot love you back again?* If God had your heart, you should have his. If you love him, he would love you, (Prov. 8:17). But silver and

gold cannot love you, your rich furniture cannot love you. Here your love is lost, and cannot be requited, nor love returned to you, but God would love you more than you could love him, and the love of Christ to you would exceed and far surpass your love to him. Come then, and no longer be enslaved to the world, nor be kept a captive by the devil by these chains of gold. I suppose a man would rather choose liberty with a poor and low condition in the world than to lie in a prison and dungeon all his days, though he were there bound with chains of gold.

6. Will the gaining of the world make you amends for what you lose, for (1) the loss of God. (2) The loss of Christ the only Redeemer. (3) The loss of the company of the angels and saints. (4) The loss of your own only and immortal soul, (Matt. 16:26). (5) The loss of your happiness, can you lose all these and yet be happy? (6) Are not these things common to the bad as well as to the good. Some are peculiar mercies, Christ's pardoning grace, title to heaven. (7) Are they not often given with a curse, and in judgment, but Christ and grace always in love and mercy?

CHAPTER 6: THE FOURTH LINK – PRESUMPTION

The fourth chain is presumption.

Another chain with which these captives are bound is *presumption, vain and false hopes of heaven.* This is the ruin of most that do miscarry forever, a groundless hope that they shall be saved forever. How few there are, be they never so ignorant of the way to heaven, but yet do hope they shall come there? They walk in the broad and common road and beaten path to hell, and yet do hope they shall get to heaven. As if a man were daily traveling towards the west, and yet were confident he should come to the east. The drunkard does hope he shall be saved. The swearer and profane, the hypocrite and unbeliever, no, who is there but that does hope for happiness? This is so strong in the worst of men that when they would set forth the certainty of a thing, they do it by this expression, as *I hope to be saved.* As if they should say, it is as true, it is as sure as it is true that I hope to be saved, and *though their hope is not a true hope, yet that they hope is true.* And the strength of this cord appears in that these hopes are the *last thing* that wicked men will part with it. When they are so sick that they perceive they must part with riches, yet they will not part with their hope of heaven, when they are so sick, that they perceive the hour is drawing in in which they must part with their *dearest friends,* yet their hope they will not part with it. And then they see they must part *with life,* yet they will not part with hope, until soul and body be parted, the soul and hope will not be parted. And *then poor captives lose their souls and hopes together.* And so with hopes of heaven they do go down to hell, and *then and there they can hope no longer.* It's one of the hardest things that ministers have to do, to beat down these false hopes of heaven in our hearers. If this were done, a great part of our work would be done. If we tell you of your misery and danger, of the wrath of God against sinners, of the torments that are prepared by a provoked God for you, yet you hope you shall escape and ward off all the threatenings of the word with these vain and groundless hopes. If we could but get these false hopes from you, then *we should begin to hope* that you might be delivered from your bondage, and escape from this captivity, in which you are so strongly held by it. No man is *faster bound in fetters,* than he that is ungodly, and yet strongly confidently hopes that he shall be saved. If you should speak with damned souls, *thousands* of them would tell you this was their ruin and their bane. Should you ask them, "Were you not told that sin would bring you to this place of torment? Were you not told *by ministers and by God himself,* that you were in the way to misery and damnation?" What would they reply? *Yes, yes, we were often told, and we were plainly told, but this was it that did undo us, we hoped it would be better with us.* Shall I then attempt to break this bond asunder? But because man can but show to you the vanity of your hopes, O that God himself would come and powerfully convince you by his word and Spirit, that your hopes are vain and groundless hopes, that you may no longer be kept in thralldom by the devil by these fetters of false hopes of heaven. I know that this is a *manifold twisted cord.* There are many things that you do bottom these hopes on, but if I shall show you from the word of God, that they are no better grounds and reasons of hope than graceless persons

Chapter 6: Presumption

might allege, and many *now in hell* once had to say, and did, as well as you, that then you will no longer suffer Satan to delude and to deceive you, and keep you as his captives in a state of bondage. Only let me ask you first, whether you will believe that *that* is true, that God speaks in his word, or will you dare to say that what is contained in the Scripture is forgery and a lie. If you say the latter, God shall shortly convince you of the truth thereof. The *flames of hell* shall shortly convince you, and the *pains and torments* that you shall shortly feel shall powerfully convince you that all these sayings of God are true. If you say the former, that God's word is true, I do not doubt to make it appear that your hope is false, if you do agree to try your hopes by the word of God, by which *you and I and all* must shortly be tried, and acquitted or condemned according to this word. I do not doubt to show that Satan has befooled you all this while. God has as plainly told you that in an unconverted state, *without faith in Christ, without repentance and reformation* you cannot be saved. This is as plain as can be spoken, and yet contrary to God's revealed will, you hope you shall be saved? Which do you think shall be proved false, *God's word* or *your hope* that is contrary to his word? Both cannot be true. Will a drunkard say, God's word is false? No, he will not. Then your hope is false. See 1 Corinthians 6:9-10, where God says plainly and positively lays down for a certain truth, and which within a few *years, or months, or weeks*, all the drunkards, whoremongers, and graceless persons in the world without exception of anyone (dying so) shall find it to be so, that they shall not inherit the kingdom of God. *Come then*, you that say you hope to be saved, as well as the most precise of you *come* and produce your reasons, and in the fear of God seriously weigh the answers that shall be given to them. Paul says,

"Know ye not that the unrighteous shall not inherit the kingdom of God? Be not deceived: neither fornicators, nor idolaters, nor adulterers, nor effeminate, nor abusers of themselves with mankind, Nor thieves, nor covetous, nor drunkards, nor revilers, nor extortioners, shall inherit the kingdom of God," (1 Corinthians 6:9-10).

1. One link in this chain of false hopes by which these captives are bound *is misapprehension and misapplication of the mercy of God. You say, God is a merciful God, and is ready to show mercy to his creature. It is true in me, there is no merit, but in God there is mercy, and God did not make his creatures to damn them, God made me, and therefore I hope that he will save me.* Is this all you have to say in such a weighty matter? Why do you think you are redeemed from your bondage, and shall be free forever from the torments of the damned? That you may no longer be bound with this chain, consider,

1. *The devil's themselves and the damned souls in hell themselves can say as much as this.* Poor damned devils know that God is a merciful God, and that he is willing to show mercy to the penitent and the humble sinner. Devils and damned souls can say that they are God's creatures, and yet notwithstanding they are miserable, and must be so forever. And this is the aggravation of their misery, that though God is merciful, yet they are forever damned. This cuts them to the heart, that a merciful God has condemned them and sentenced them down to eternal torments. What is that to them, that God is merciful in himself and shows mercy to others, if he is not merciful to them? And *what is it to you*, that God is so, if you by reason of your continuance in an unregenerate state, shall never be benefited by his mercy? I know that there is a difference between the damned in hell and wicked men on earth. The

damned in hell are past a possibility of mercy, but are you not so? They shall have no more tenders of mercy, which you yet have, but then you must repent and be converted, which they did not, or else you shall have no saving benefit by God's mercy as they did not have.

2. *God might be infinite in mercy, though you* (and thousands such as you are) *perish in your bondage, and are forever damned.* What a proud blasphemous thought is this that God should not be merciful, except he take you *reeking* in your sins, except he take you off your alehouse bench, and put you into heaven. The greatness of God's mercy is not manifested so much by the *number* of the persons that shall be saved as by the *way and method* by which he saves them. If God had saved but *one man* out of all the many millions of mankind, without his own desert, and contrary to it, by the death of his own Son, it would have been a plain demonstration of the mercy of God. Must you measure the mercy of God by your being saved, or not saved, while you walk contrary to his Law and to his revealed will? This is, as if a *malefactor* that for murder has deserved death, and is to be tried for his life, yet hopes he shall escape, because the judge is a *merciful man.* When notwithstanding, the judge proceeds to pass a sentence of death on him, you will all acknowledge that he might be a very merciful man, and that the prisoner was a fool, from the mercy of the judge to be confident that he should escape the execution due to him for the violation of the law. So it is in this case, which is easy to apply.

3. *God is just and true, as well as merciful and gracious*, and why might you not *fear* that God will damn you, because he is a just God, as well as *hope* that he will save you because he is a merciful God? You do not conceive of God aright, when

you consider him to be merciful without justice, and to be gracious without truth, there are both in God. This merciful God has said, "Except you repent and turn from sin, you shall find no mercy from him." And what shall become of God's truth, if contrary to his word he should save you without repentance, and while you go on in your sinful ways? Must God falsify his word to save your soul, *never hope for it, for he will never do it.* Where God proclaims his mercy to the penitent, he does also declare his justice and his jealousy, and his fixed resolution that the guilty shall not go free, (Exod. 34:6-7), and that he is full of fury to the wicked, as of mercy to the godly, and that as he reserves a crown for the one, so also wrath for the other, (Nahum 1:2-3).

4. *Though God is merciful, yet he propounds conditions in the gospel*, which you must come up to if you will be partakers of his mercy. And God is resolved that if you will not have mercy on the terms of mercy that you shall never have it. When you shall come to put in your claim for mercy, "Lord, have mercy on me, for you are a gracious God," yes, may God say, "And so I am, and those that have repented and believed shall find me to be so, but did I not also tell you what manner of person you should have been, holy, humble, and repenting, if you would be saved by my mercy? But that you would not be. Therefore, *now* I have no mercy for you." God may say to you, "Did I ever promise you or any other, that I would save you, or them without repentance and faith in Christ my son? Did I ever promise that I would pardon the impenitent? That I would save the unbelieving that finally persevere therein? If I have, produce my words, allege my promise, *when, and where, and by whom* did I ever make you such a promise? And if I have not, as indeed I have not promised any such thing, why were you so vainly

Chapter 6: Presumption

confident of your mercy? Therefore, *take your answer and be gone?* For I tell you I will have no mercy on you, (Luke 13:25-27). Mercy itself will not save you, but in the way of mercy propounded in the gospel."

5. Where you say, God did make you, therefore he will save you. Consider, *the vilest sinner in the world on this account should go to heaven,* yes, every one of them. The whoremonger whom you yourself will condemn might plead this as well as you. And so you will make the way to heaven broader than God ever made it. Moreover, if you had continued such a one as God made, he would then have made you happy indeed forever. God made you holy and upright, but you have rebelled against him. God made you a *creature,* but he did not make you a *drunkard.* He did not make you a *worldling,* nor a *liar.* Therefore, let God's creature be holy, and God will not damn his creature. But if you are a drunkard, or a hypocrite, and God shall damn the *drunkard or the hypocrite.* What will become of *God's creature?* God does peremptorily answer this, and I will give it to you in his own words, "It is a people of no understanding. Therefore, he that made them will not have mercy on them, and he that formed them will show them no favor," (Isa. 27:11). Is not this directly contrary to the reason of your hope? Will you then plead this no more, while you continue in your sin, and not let Satan keep you bound with this cord any longer? If you do, remember it has been told to you, that this is but a sandy foundation of your hope, that you shall have the everlasting mercy that shall be shown to God's redeemed ones, that are indeed delivered from their bondage and captivity.

2. Another link in this chain of false hopes by which captives are bound is a *strong (though false) persuasion of*

salvation by the death of Christ the Redeemer. If you ask many carnal, ignorant and ungodly persons why they persuade themselves that they shall be saved, they will tell you, because *Christ died for sinners, and I am a sinner* (says one), *God help me, as all men are, yes, I am the chief of sinners, and therefore, I hope it shall go well with me.* And so will a second say, and a third, and *multitudes* will give no better account, without care or knowledge of applying the death of Christ to them and the virtue and power of it, for the killing of their sins. And thus the *very means* for the redeeming of captives is abused to make their bonds stronger, and keep them faster bound in their captivity.

By way of concession it is granted, (1) that *the death of Christ, and the satisfaction made to the justice of God by it is the only meritorious cause of man's redemption from his bondage and of salvation*, and whoever is saved, is saved by Christ's death, for there is no other Savior nor Redeemer besides him, (Acts 4:12). And if Christ had not died, we would certainly have been captives forever without redemption. (2) It is true that *this Redeemer is offered to all where the gospel is preached*, none are excluded from the offers of grace and pardon, and benefits of redemption, and his death shall be sufficient and effectual for deliverance from bondage, and making of them free that obey his call, and receive him as *Lord Redeemer*, as offered in the gospel, (Acts 10:43; John 3:16). But yet that you might through your own mistake be the more enthralled by the means of redemption, and be the faster bound by the misunderstanding of the way of salvation by the death of Christ. *Consider,*

1. If this were enough to prove your redemption and salvation, because Christ died for sinners, and you

acknowledge yourselves to be such, *then the damned souls in hell might have hope of being delivered and saved.* For they know that Christ died for sinners, and they are *now sensible* that they are sinners and miserable. The *pains* they feel convince them that they are sinners I know (as I have already said) that there is a difference between the state of devils and damned souls, and of sinners on earth, *Christ* is preached to the one, and not to the other, *freedom* from bondage is *possible* to one but not to the other, *mercy* does entreat, and the *Spirit* does strive, and *patience* does wait on the one, but not on the other. *Mercy and patience is done with them forever.* No more asking them, what? Will you have Christ now? And will you be pardoned now? Which yet through mercy is not your condition. But yet as to the ground of your plea for redemption and salvation by Christ (before alleged) [*Christ died for sinners and you are sinners*] what is the difference? All men on earth and the damned in hell that ever heard of Christ might say as much. And is it not matter of great astonishment to sober serious men, to see poor sinners bound so fast in a captive state with this vain confidence of being set free by Christ, and yet can say no more than damned souls might say that they are sinners, and Christ died for sinners.

2. Consider *that not all that are sinners shall be saved by the death of Christ.* Christ has died, yet thousands shall forever be tormented, (Matt. 7:13-14). And the damnation of many shall be greater than it would have been if Christ had never suffered.

3. *Know and understand that the benefits of redemption, and the completing of all in salvation at the last is propounded by God in the gospel unconditionally*, and why then should you be so confident, when you have not come up

into the condition? There is *pardon* to be had by the blood of Christ, but there is a *condition*, without which you shall never be pardoned, (Acts 10:43). There is salvation by Christ, but there is a *condition*, without which you shall never be saved, (John 3:16, 36; Mark 16:16; Acts 16:30). There is *justification* to be had by the blood of Christ, but remember there is still a *condition* without which you shall never be justified, (Rom. 5:1). All along in the word of God, *offers and grants* of pardon, deliverance from hell, and the curse of the law, *offers* and *grants* of salvation and eternal life are made *conditionally* if you believe, and if you repent, and if you are converted and born again, but none else. Christ did not die that sinners *merely as sinners* should be saved, for then *all sinners* should be saved, and that which is the *reason of men's condemnation* should be a *qualification of men's salvation*, but Christ died that *believing sinners* might be saved, and *repenting and returning sinners* might be saved. Christ did die that unholy ones might be made holy and *so be saved*, that unbelievers might believe, and *so be saved*, and not that unholy and impenitent and unbelieving persons *living and dying so* should have salvation by his death. Know therefore, *O vain man*, that if you had a *thousand souls*, they should all be damned, though Christ has died, except you do believe, repent, and be converted to God. For the *effusion* or shedding of the blood of Christ on the cross saves no man's soul, without the *application* of it to the conscience. And faith in Christ, and regeneration, and holiness, and repairing of the image of God in the soul are necessary to salvation *in their place*, as the death of Christ is necessary *in its place*, and *for its end*. As when many persons are in bondage, and are taken captives, that cannot give a ransom for themselves, the *King's son* pays it down for them, but the king and his Son do propound certain conditions to the captives, that if they will acknowledge him to be their Redeemer, and will become his servants and his subjects, and be obedient to his laws, they shall have the benefit of the ransom, but none else. Now so many as shall refuse these *conditions*, must remain, and die, and perish in their fetters, though a sufficient ransom were given for redemption. So it is in this case, which is easy to apply.

I beseech you therefore, sirs, do not any longer flatter and deceive yourselves with such groundless hopes of being delivered by the death of Christ from your slavery and bondage, without faith in him, and repentance for your sin. These things that I am now preaching, and you are hearing are of *everlasting concern* to your souls. And I desire to preach as one that does believe, I must give an account to God, what doctrine I deliver, and that you would hear with that seriousness and diligent attention, as those should do, that do believe you must give an account to God at the great day, for what you hear, and how you do obey it. I charge you there *in the name of the great eternal God*, whose truths I do declare to you, that you do not here hope forward for deliverance from hell and wrath to come, though Christ has died, except you do believe in him, become new creatures, forsake your sin, be sanctified and made holy, and love him above all, and count all things but dross in comparison of the excellency of Jesus Christ. That you do not continue *drunkards*, and yet hope you shall be saved, that you do not continue to love your sins, and the world more than Christ, or remain unholy and unconverted, and yet think or hope that Christ's death shall save your souls. If you do, and if you will still do so, let *God be a witness* for me, and let all those *that fear* God in the congregation be witnesses for me, and let the *consciences* of these captives themselves be witnesses for me, that I have plainly from the word of God given warning to you, that you do not perish by this deceit. *Bear witness* that I do declare that those that have been *drunkards, swearers, profane, liars, hypocrites*, if they do repent and turn, become holy and believing persons, they *may*, they *shall* be saved by the death of Christ, but if they shall continue still in sin, and live and die such, a crucified Christ will not save you. Let *believing parents* bear me witness against their wicked and ungodly *children*, and believing *children* against their ungodly *parents*. Let believing *husbands* bear me witness against their unbelieving *wives*, and believing *wives* against their unbelieving *husbands*. Let believing *masters* bear me witness against their unbelieving *servants*, and believing *servants* against their unbelieving *masters*, that all without *exception* and respect of persons, not having repentance for sin, nor faith in Christ, that are not holy, nor converted before they die, shall be eternally damned, and perish in their bonds and fetters, though Christ has died to redeem and save holy, humble, repenting, and believing sinners.

Alas *poor captive sinners!* What will you do, and where will you go, when this Redeemer shall come to judgment? When all shall be raised out of their graves, and stand before the bar of God? To whom will you appeal? And from whom will you expect mercy and salvation? *I think* I hear these *prisoners at the bar, crying, begging, pleading, Lord Jesus, save us! Lord Jesus, open to us! Lord Jesus, now glorify us with yourself, save us, O save us now from yonder places of torment, from yonder flaming fire, from yonder lake of burning brimstone! O do not send us down to yonder dreadful place, for we trusted in your merits, and hoped to be saved because you had died!* I think I hear Jesus the Judge reply to the *prisoners* at the bar, "No, O no,

Chapter 6: Presumption

there is no room for you in heaven." There is *no entrance* for ungodly men into the holy place, there is *no mansion* for any such in the kingdom of my Father. *Who* bid you to trust me for mercy, without believing on me? *Who* bid you to hope for heaven because I was crucified, without holiness and repentance? Had you any warrant from me in my work to do so? Or did my ministers whom I sent unto you tell you for me, that you may be saved by my death, though you did not repent, believe, nor were converted? Did they? Which is he? What is his name? Lo, here they stand, point *him* to me that preached such doctrine to you. My ministers come forth, what do you say against the *prisoners* at the bar? Lord we told them in your name that there was a ransom paid for captives by your blessed self, and that you were willing that they should have the everlasting benefit thereof. And we studied for them, prayed for them, and preached to them your sufferings and your death for sinners, and begged and entreated them to come to you. And when we did not prevail one day, we prepared and preached the next, and so we continued to do, as long as they lived and until you called us from that work by death. *But did you ever tell them that they should be saved by my death, though they continued in their sins, though they had no faith in me, though they were not sanctified nor converted.*

O no, our blessed Lord, we never did, we never did, *there* they stand before you, they cannot say we ever preached such doctrine to them. But on the contrary, that we told them from your word which we made the *rule and matter* of our sermons, and turned them to the places where you have said, "without holiness" they should not see your face with comfort, (Heb. 12:14). We bid them to turn to Mark 16:16, where you told them yourself, that "he that does not believe will be damned," and to many more such declarations of your mind to sinners. Lord *there stands one* that used to hear me, and he cannot deny it. And *there stands another* that was used to hear me, and turned to the chapter and the verse, and turned it down, as if he would have observed what you have declared. Lord, *there he stands*, he cannot deny it. Yes, Lord, here is a *whole cluster* of them standing together that were wont to hear me, and there is not one among them all that can deny that they were told of what they now find. And *here are those* that believed on you through our preaching of your word, that can say and witness for us that we told them of the necessity of converting grace, and faith in you. In the same *sermon* that we preached that you did die for sinners, we also told them that they must take you for their Lord, and obey your laws, and resign their *hearts and wills, and love*, and all to you, but they would not do it. But they never did it. This is the evidence that we give against the *prisoners at the bar. Come then you captives, is this true, or is it not?* Yes, Lord, our *consciences* do compel us, to acknowledge that your ministers declared such things to us. *Did they do so?* Why then did you not believe them? God will get you gone. God will get you down to your deserved torments. Come here, you my glorious angels, take the prisoners at the bar, that in their lifetime were fettered and bound with chains of sin. Now *come* here, and take them, bind them hand and foot, and cast them into utter darkness. Drive them from my presence. *Away with them, away with them. Come* you damned devils, you took them captive and kept them in their sinful bondage. I would have redeemed them, and knocked off their fetters from them, but they would not hearken to me, and now I will not hearken to them. *Come* take them then, and drag them down to the place of punishment, *where you and they shall be forever.*

Oh *woeful souls! Poor wretched sinners! Ah poor condemned prisoners!* How do they tremble? How do they hang down their heads? How are their countenances changed? What hideous outcries? What doleful lamentations will there be at that day, and especially by those that hoped for heaven, but their hopes are disappointed? *I think* I hear them say, are all our hopes come to this? Is this the end of all our confidence? We were prisoners to the devil and our lusts, we might have been made free, *woe to us that we were ever born*, that we did fool ourselves, and that these *then tempting,* and *now tormenting* devils should so much fool us, contrary to the plain declarations of the will of Christ. We should so confidently hope for life and for salvation by him, while we did refuse him for our Lord, and yield obedience to him. O *now* we are ashamed of our hope, of our vain and foolish hope, yet thus it is, we *were* deceived, and we *are now* disappointed. Now *farewell* Christ forever, now *farewell* heaven forever, and now *farewell* hope forever. We did hope, but now we can hope no longer, but now we can hope no more forever. *Farewell* all you holy, blessed angels, *you* shall be rejoicing forever, while *we* shall be sorrowing forever. *Farewell* all you saints of God, *you* that are the Lord's redeemed, that were once captives as well as we, but *you* were redeemed by the blood of Christ, and were sanctified and are now saved forever. *You* will rejoice, but *we* must mourn, *you* are blessed, but *we* are cursed, *you* shall be with God and Christ your Redeemer forever, while *we* shall be with the devil and his angels forever. *Farewell, farewell, adieu, adieu,* to all eternity.

Beloved hearers, if this shall be the doleful end of vain and groundless hopes of unwarranted and unscriptural confidence in the death of Christ, without faith and sanctifying grace, be kept no longer as captives bound by this chain of false hopes of heaven.

3. Another link in this chain of false hopes by which these captives are bound, is, *that they have oftentimes great trouble of conscience and inward terrors of mind after they have committed sin.* "I have," says one, "been troubled for my oaths, and cried 'God forgive me,'" and "if I have been drunk," says another, "I have been troubled for it, sometimes it breaks my sleep, and sometimes I cannot eat in peace, nor think of my sin but my heart is filled with horror at the remembrance of it." And therefore I hope that I am redeemed by Christ, and got loose from my bondage state, and that God will have mercy on me, and will save my soul." I *answer,*

1. *False repentance is a strengthening of false hopes, and many times the more the sinner is troubled for his sin, the faster he is bound in his sinful captive state.* The more tears do fall from your eyes, the faster your fetters are locked on your soul, because as true repentance makes way for a well-grounded peace of conscience, and for solid comfort, so a false and counterfeit repentance afterwards makes the sinner more secure, and does strengthen his mistake concerning his spiritual condition, he has *sinned,* and he has *sorrowed,* and how he thinks *all is well.* And the devil has him faster in his hold than he had before.

2. *Terrors of conscience for sin, though great and grievous,* so much so that you are restless and weary of your life, are *no argument that as a captive you are made free.* Have you ever been so much troubled as Cain was? Or have you ever been

so filled with amazing horrors as Judas was? And yet these were captives to the devil still, and are bound in chains of sin, and guilt, and punishment, to *this day*, and so shall be forever. And who has greater terrors, reprovings and reproaches from their own consciences, than the damned in hell? And these terrors in your soul and conscience, might be the forerunners and beginning of those hellish horrors you shall be filled with in another world.

3. But *what are your terrors and your tears, the agonies and anguish of your heart, without an inward change?* What are all these legal fits of sorrow, while you are the same man in sinning still, and your love the same to your sin. And when the temptation comes, your course and practice is the same? If you should *wear* the skirt from off your knees by going often to confess your sin, and *weep* yourself blind, and *pine* away with sorrow. Yet if your heart does secretly like your sin, and you still are not inwardly renewed, nor receive, not close with Christ by faith. Whatever your apprehensions are of your good condition, you are still a captive to the devil, especially when once in a while you seem *with sorrow to lament your sin*, and another while you do with *pleasure and delight commit* the sin lamented, while you commit the sin, and then confess it, while you confess it, and go on again to commit it. And so like a slave indeed you run around in the devil's mill between confession and commission of your sins, whereas in a true penitent there is the renovation of the heart, and the reformation of the life, a *loathing* and a *leaving* of the sin lamented, (Ezek. 36:31; 18:30-31; Isa. 57:7; Joel 2:12-13).

4. Another link in this chain of false hopes, by which these captives are bound is in *that they have good meanings, and good wishes and desires. And though they cannot*

discourse as others can, nor have those gifts that others have, yet they thank God their hearts are good, and ever were even from their childhood, and though they cannot utter it themselves, yet they have it in their hearts. So the devil keeps some in this fetter and this bond. But towards the breaking of it, *consider,*

1. *Many have gone to hell with such good meanings in their hearts, and with such good wishes in their mouths,* as *Balaam* for one, "Let me die the death of the righteous, and let my last end be like his," (Num. 23:10). Who would not wish to be happy forever? And who would not wish to be freed from eternal misery, pain, and torment? But these things are not obtained with such lazy wishes. Neither do you approve of them in your idle servants, that sit still and wish their work was done.

2. *But can your meanings be good, in many of your wicked acts, and in your sinful neglects?* What good meaning is it to keep Christ out of your heart? To profane God's Sabbaths? What good meaning do you have in neglecting to make peace with God? In not seeking after grace and fitness for heaven?

3. *If your meanings were good, this does not make your action good,* nor your life good. And can it then prove your condition to be good?

4. *If your heart was good, your life would be so too.* The life indeed might be good before men, where the heart is bad before God. But if the heart is good before God, the life will be good before men, "for a good tree brings forth good fruit," (Matt. 7:17-18). And not seeing the badness of your hearts is evidence that yet they are not good. And the more you justify the goodness of your hearts in the neglect of your duty is the

clearer demonstration that yet they are not good, and that your heart, which you vainly think is the best part of you, is indeed the worst of all, (Jer. 17:9-10). You had a good heart ever since you were born! Then there has been a good devil ever since he sinned, and when he ceased to be good.

5. Whereas you say, *you have good things in your heart, though you cannot express them with your tongue.* Why is your heart so full of good? And is it so locked up there, that there is no vent for it? What! Neither by *works* nor *words?* Neither by lip nor life? A likely matter! If you are pinched with *hunger,* you have enough words to express the sense of what you lack, and if you are *sick,* you have enough words to express the sense of your pain. When the *physician* comes and asks after the state of your body, you can quickly reply, *O sick, sick,* sir, *I am exceedingly sick. I am in pain, in pain.* Where? Here in this part, and in this. *My back, my bowels, my head, my heart,* is full of pain. But if a *minister* come and inquire into your spiritual state, you reply. Truly sir, I have good things in my mind and in my heart, but I cannot express them to you. What! Not at all? What! Nothing of this good boasted of? No, not in broken language? But if we follow you to your shops, there you want no words, there your tongues go glib. Who have words at your command more than you? You can talk roundly of the world, of your goods, and your estates, of your furniture and apparel. But in the things of God you are mute. This is plain, it is not for want of words in these, but for want of a work of God on your hearts. Therefore, do not let the devil keep you any longer bound with this chain, a vain conceit of the goodness of your heart, your wishings, and your meanings.

5. Another link in this chain of false hopes by which these captives are bound is on the contrary, in that *they have*

strong parts, great knowledge in the things of God, are very full of good discourse. For the devil has several fetters for his several prisoners, and several chains for several captives, various ways and wiles to keep them in captivity. And this is not the meanest nor the weakest, when men take *gifts for grace,* and *common grace for special.* But towards the cutting of this chain, consider:

There might be *notional knowledge* of the things of God, where a man never had any *experimental taste and relish* of them. A man that never yet repented might be able to tell you what repentance is. And a man that is not converted might tell you much of the method of the Spirit in the converting of a sinner. Many can *talk* of God, that never *tasted* any sweetness in him. And many can discourse of heaven, that shall never enter into heaven. The head might be full of knowledge, when the heart is empty of grace. It might talk of *faith*, of the *nature* of it, of the *actings* of it, of the *excellency* of it, of the *necessity and effects* of it, and yet have no faith. And so of love, and other graces, and yet have no love, nor any other grace. The greater is your knowledge, the greater is your sin, and the greater will be your misery if it is separated from practice and obedience (Luke 12:47-48).

Thus you have heard what a strong bond *false hope* of heaven is, and on what *grounds* it is built, and by what *reasons* it is strengthened, and *how* they are removed. What do you say now? Will you continue still bound with this cord, and still be kept by it in your captivity? I doubt that many of you will. *Drunkards*, for all this that has been said, will you hope for heaven and salvation still. And *swearers* and *profane* persons will go on in their sinful course, and yet hope still for heaven and eternal life. Therefore, because this fetter is so strong, if

Chapter 6: Presumption

possible to knock it off from these captive sinners, answer me to these few following questions.

1. *What if Christ himself in person were now among you, and preaching to you, and telling you with his own mouth, that these alleged grounds of your hopes of heaven, and redemption by his blood, were not found nor warranted, would you after this hope you are redeemed, and shall be saved?* If Christ were visibly present, and you should hear him with your own ears telling you that the drunkard is a captive to the devil, and shall not be saved. Would you say, no, we are not in bondage to the devil, or our sins, and therefore *will* hope we are redeemed and shall be saved? Would you believe Christ himself? Or would you not? If you would not, how shall I hope you will hearken to my words? If you say you would believe him, why then will you not believe what Christ has indeed *already* spoken, and left recorded in his word? The same doctrine that Christ preached in person in the world is faithfully recorded in the gospel. In his sermon that he preached on the mount, he tells you, that "unless your righteousness exceeds the righteousness of the scribes and Pharisees, you shall in no way enter into the kingdom of heaven," (Matt. 5:20). And does the righteousness of gross sinners, yes or close hypocrites, either exceed the righteousness of the *Pharisees* and the *scribes*, who walked so strictly, that many would have judged, if but *two* men should be saved, the *scribe* should be one, and the *Pharisee* the other? What Christ's doctrine was, see again, (Luke 13:3-5; Mark 16:16; Matt. 18:3). And yet when Christ tells you, *unless you repent, you will perish*, and *unless you believe, you shall be damned*, and *unless you are converted, you will not enter into the kingdom of God.* You do still remain captives, and do you not repent, nor believe,

nor are converted, and yet will you hope you are freemen, and shall be saved? The truth is, if you do not believe Christ's ministers preaching Christ's own words, neither would you believe Christ himself, "He that hears you, hears me, and he that despises you, despises me, and he that despises me, despises him that sent me," (Luke 10:16). Not to hear is to despise, and whom do you despise when you do not hear and obey the doctrine preached according to the Scripture? Is it *poor mortal* men? No, but you despise Christ, and God himself. Believe me then, or rather believe Christ himself, that tells you, without converting grace you shall be damned, and except you are converted, do not hope that you are delivered out of your captivity, or that you shall be saved, and so be fooled by the devil, and by it be still kept in bondage by him.

2. *What if God should send an angel from heaven to you, and tell you while you are a drunkard, swearer, profane, a liar, an hypocrite, a worldling, are unsanctified, you are a captive to the devil, and abiding so, shall not be saved?* Would you after such a message from God by a glorious angel, still hope you are made free, and shall be saved? Or would you *then* leave your sins, and look after grace, and make it your business to get out of bondage? Why, if an angel should come from heaven, he would preach *this* doctrine to you, the *very same* that is contained in the word of God, or else a blessed angel would be a cursed creature, (Gal. 1:8). But behold, you have a surer and more certain way of knowing the mind of God, and that is the Scripture, (2 Peter 1:17-19). For if an angel came from heaven, you would be doubting whether he came from God or not. But that the Scripture is from God, we have plain, full, and undeniable reasons to believe, and the truth is, if you will not

Chapter 6: Presumption

believe the Scripture, neither would you believe an angel that should come from heaven.

3. *What if you could with safety draw near to the gates of hell and take a view of those thousands there in restless torments, that lived once as now you do, and were persuaded that they were redeemed and made free, and that they should be saved, as confidently as you now are. Would you still continue in your sinful state and course of life, and yet hope, after such a sight as this?* That though you saw so many thousands damned before you for the *same* sins as you live in, would you yet be confident that you shall be delivered? *Poor sinner!* What shall I do for you? What shall I say to you? Will nothing convince you, nor awaken you on this side of the flames of hell? Will you *believe* none of these truths, until you shall *feel* them all made good on you? Will you be more brutish than your very beast, which you cannot force nor drive into a burning fire? And yet when you are told there is a fire that is kindled, into which the slaves of sin and Satan shall be cast, you will voluntarily walk in that way that leads you to it? What if God should take you to some place, and bid you to *stand and see* so many millions rolling in a lake of brimstone, and bid you to *stand and hearken and hear* their groans and hideous howlings, their doleful outcries, and dolorous complaints, *one* confessing, God has justly damned me for my drunkenness and my oaths, and *another*, I am here tormented for my Sabbath-breaking, and pleasing of my flesh, and *another*, I am suffering in these flames for my hypocrisy and unbelief, and a *thousand thousands* making of the same complaints. After you had heard such things as these, would you remain a drunkard, a swearer, a Sabbath-breaker, a hypocrite, and an unbeliever, a captive in your bonds of sin, and yet persuade yourself that you are free,

and that you shall never be one of the number of this cursed crew? *I think* such sights and hearings of such things, should awaken and alarm you. Why, tell me then, why should you not believe the *True Eternal God*, as well as your own *eyes* and *ears*? Such are *there* that died without repentance and faith, that died in their bondage state, and the *same* God that has already damned them, does also threaten you for the *same* sins with the *same* damnation, and yet shall Satan still keep you bound with this false hope of a better place? O! Let him not do it, as you love your soul, and as you would escape this place, let him no longer do it.

4. *What if God should send one of your acquaintances and companions that has been in hell a year or two, a month or two, one that you were wont to swear and swagger with, to drink with and carouse, whose corps not long since you followed it to the grave, whose soul when separated from the body, went down to hell, should come to you and say, I was wont to be merry and jovial in your company. With you I was accustomed to game and sport, and waste and spend my precious time, and I hoped I should be saved when I died, as now you do. But woe is me, I find I was mistaken to my everlasting shame and sorrow. I find I was deceived. I find, I find I did but flatter and delude myself. I would not believe it, but now I find it. I would not believe it, but now I feel it. Ministers did warn me of this place, and told me I was going there, but I would not be convinced until I came to hell. I still hoped I should go to heaven, but now I am convinced, alas, when it is too late to be converted, I am at last convinced. Believe me,* though a damned soul, *believe me, the word of God is true, the threatenings of God are true, and what your ministers preach out of God's word concerning sin, and misery*

by sin is all true. Believe me now that I have been in hell ever since the day I died, that the bond-slaves of the devil, that die in their captivity, do all go down to this dark and dreadful dungeon. If one of your neighbors not long since departed and damned should appear to you in this way in your chamber in the silent night, and bring you such tidings as these, would you believe him and repent, and refuse from then forwards to be a servant and slave to the devil? It may be that you think you should believe this doctrine then, and take warning and reform and mend your ways. Tell me then, should not the *true eternal God of heaven* be believed *sooner, rather more* than a *damned soul* in hell? But it is certain that if you will not believe the Scriptures nor the ministers of God that preach the truths of God to you, nor repent and turn from the drudgery of the devil to the service of the Lord, neither would you do it if one came to you from the dead, *to the end,* (Luke 16:27).

5. *What if you had been in hell yourself a month or two, and felt the pains and torments there, and God should let you out again, and put you in the same capacity as now you are in, and place you again under the same means and ministry as now you do enjoy, and the same doctrine should be preached to you, and the same offers of Christ and pardon, of heaven and eternal life as now you hear? Would you then hearken to our doctrine, and renounce the devil's service, and beg and pray that God would knock off your fetters and your chains, and of a slave of Satan, make you a willing servant of your blessed and living God?* Or would you still live as now you do, and hope again on the same grounds as now, that you should not be cast the second time into that place of torment? O then why will you not believe that God cannot lie, as well as your own experience?

God will never do *this*. He will never try you again, nor set you in this life again. *Once* you are in hell, you are *forever* there. God will not give you a *second life*, to mend what was amiss in your living on earth. If you think you should be more careful, if God should try you after he had damned you, that you may not be damned again. Why should you not be as careful now that you may not be damned at all?

What then *poor captive sinner!* Will you after all this that has been said go on in sin, and yet hope you shall do well? Or shall the devil still keep you in captivity, and hold you fast in this bond and chain of a false persuasion, that your state is good, and groundless hopes that you shall be saved? I am afraid he will, O I do greatly fear he will. *Poor prisoner!* What do you think of? What ails you? Why are you no more concerned at the hearing of these things? Will you still remain in the fool's paradise? Why do I preach, and why do you come and hear, if you will not regard what is spoken to you from the *word of God*, in the *name of God*? O how hard a thing it is, to *stand* and *view* so many souls, and think after all the study, pains, prayer, and preaching, for you and to you, *so many* should still be in the devil's fetters, and are going in chains to the prison of hell, and bound fast in sin to a place of everlasting torments? O how shall I do to bear the thoughts of your damnation? O it is a *burden*, it is a *burden*, it is indeed a h*eavy burden* to my soul to think that any of you should be damned, that you should go from here to hell, from a place of *solemn worship* to a place of *torment* and of *blasphemy*. Do you think it is not enough to break a poor minister's heart, to preach and labor that your bonds may be broken, and your souls escape and be set at liberty, and after all you are still in fetters? Were it not that *some* do hearken and obey, were it not that *some* give great grounds of hope that they are leaving off the devil's service, and that their chains are broken, it would be a *sore temptation, to preach no more*. But alas! Though some are set at liberty, what shall we do for the rest that still remain in bonds? Especially in this, that is so strong, a *false persuasion that you are already free*, and false hopes that you shall be saved forever. Sirs, the stronger your *false hopes are*, the greater is poor ministers' *true and real sorrow*. And the more you *hope* for heaven on such slender grounds, the more we do *despair* of being instruments to help you out. The more *confident* we see you to be that you are not in bondage, the more *discouragement* it is unto us. For if we set forth the misery of these captives, we love our labor as to *you*, because you think you are not the persons, if we exhort and direct you to look after liberty, *as to you* we lose our labor, because you are persuaded (strongly though falsely) that you are free already. Whereas, if you did see yourselves in chains, and were sensible of your bonds, there were more hopes that we might prevail with you to receive of a Redeemer. O that God would break this bond! O that God would open your eyes, that you may see that you are captives, and not be so vainly confident that you are made free! O that my head were waters, and mine eyes fountains of tears, that I might lament night and day the woeful state of these captives that are on their way to hell, and that think they are in the way to heaven. But let me leave this particular, by leaving this with such *presuming captives*, that if you *will* hope, while your eyes are *open*. Yet when *death* shall *close* your eyes, you shall *hope no more*. Let me commend to you the serious study of *three* places of Scripture, and I will proceed to the next. The first is, "The hypocrites' hope shall perish, whose hope shall be cut off, and whose trust shall be a spider's web," (Job 8:13-14). If your hope perishes, shall not your souls perish too? If your hope is cut off, will not your souls be cut short of heaven hoped for? If your hope is as a spider's web, can it be a sure hope? Can the spider's web stand before broom? God at furthest with the *broom of death will sweep your hope away.*

The second is, "But the eyes of the wicked shall fail, and they shall not escape, and their hope shall be as the giving up of the ghost," (Job 11:20). You *poor captive*, look for heaven, but your eyes shall fail before you have it. You look for happiness, but you shall look your eyes out, before (without being made free by Christ) you shall enjoy it. You hope you shall *escape* wrath and hell, but you shall not escape. It is the true, infallible God that says you shall *not escape*, and your hope shall be as the *giving up of the ghost*, in these respects:

1. *A man is unwilling to give up the ghost.* It is the last thing he does. You are unwilling to give up your false hopes of heaven. Except God prevents it, it will be the *last* thing you will do.

2. A man *must* give up the ghost, though he never is so unwilling to do it. He would not die, but he *must.* You *must* at last give over hoping. Though you keep this hope until you die, yet then you shall hope no more. *It is as impossible for you to keep these hopes forever, as it is for you to live on earth forever.*

3. A man that gives up the ghost, by *all the power on earth cannot be called to life again.* When your soul and body part, then your soul and hope shall part, and you shall lose both hope and soul together. The parting of the soul and body is a sad parting, but the parting of the soul and hope is a sadder parting. And when your soul has parted with its hopes at death, hope shall never return again. Your soul parted from your body shall return to it again, but not your hope to your soul. Your

Chapter 6: Presumption

body falls and shall rise again, but *there shall never be a resurrection of your hope.*

Some translate these words this way, *and their hopes shall perish at the expiration of the soul.* The sinner shall breathe out his soul and hope at once. These words (*the giving up of the ghost*) are but two words in the Hebrew text, and the *one* signifies not only the *soul,* but also the *breath,* or a *puff of wind,* and the *other,* signifies to *blow,* which imports that the hope of wicked men, the devil's captives, shall be but as a *puff of wind,* or as *the blast of a man's mouth.* And *one* of the words signifies sometimes to *grieve and so be fed.* So the hope of these captives shall end in sorrow and sadness. It shall make him *sad, to puff, and blow,* that he trusted for such great and weighty things as heaven and salvation on such slight and slender grounds. Again, the Hebrew word has another meaning, to *despise, and loathe, and nauseate a thing.* This may teach us that though these captives do now think well of their hope, yet at last they shall *loathe it* and *abhor it,* as a man will do some rotten and unsavory thing. Now you will not loathe your *sins,* but hereafter you shall loathe your very *hope.* Now you will not loathe yourselves for your iniquity, but hereafter you shall for your folly.

The third text is, "For what is the hope of the hypocrite, though he has gained, when God takes away his soul?" (Job 27:28). Yes, what is it indeed? You have gained riches, and you have gained in a way of hypocrisy (which men could not judge of) credit and esteem, a name of a good, and holy, zealous man! But what is this gain, or what is your hope, though you have gained the name of being religious, when God takes away your soul? From where? *From your body.* To where? *To eternal torments.* What will be your hope then? And will you still be bound by this chain? This has had a greater proportion of time than can be allowed to the rest, because I judge it to be one of the strongest bonds in which multitudes are carried captive to the hellish prison.

CHAPTER 7:
THE FIFTH LINK – DESPAIR

The fifth chain by which captives are held to despair.

Another chain by which some captives are fast bound is contrary to the former, a *despairing of mercy*. Not only a despairing in a man's self, seeing an utter inability to help himself, *this is necessary*, but a despairing of pardon and salvation notwithstanding the *mercy of God*, and the *merit of Christ*, through which pardon and salvation is tendered to them. The devil uses *various*, yes, *contrary* means and methods to hold fast sinners in their bonds. If he can, he will keep them from a sight and sense of sin and misery by it. If he cannot, but God opens a sinner's eyes and awakens his conscience, the devil will set out his sins with all the *aggravations* of them, but endeavors to keep them from the *sight of Christ*, *sometimes* persuading sinners that their sins are *not so great*. But they may do well enough, *sometimes* that they are *so heinous*, that there is *no hope*, nor help for them. *Sometimes* he blinds their eyes that they see no need of a Savior. *Sometimes* he shows them their sin in a *multiplying or magnifying glass*, that a Savior can do them no good. And the poor captive is held and kept from Christ the Redeemer either way, though it is more rare, the sinners do *despair*, but it is more frequent and more ordinary for them to *presume*, as it was said of Saul and David, "Saul slew his thousands, but David his ten thousands," (1 Sam. 18:7). So we might say, if *thousands* perish in their captivity by *despair*, there are ten thousands many times told, that perish by *presumption* and false hopes of heaven. Sometimes the sinner cries out with Cain, "My sin is greater than can be forgiven," (Gen. 4:13). And with Judas is tempted to despair, and destroy himself.

But that the poor captive that is convinced of his sins, might not be kept from Christ the Redeemer by this bond, I shall speak three things towards the breaking of it. Do you then cry out in the anguish of your soul, O *the greatness of my sins, they are scarlet, crimson sins! O the number of my sins, they cannot be reckoned up! There is not a viler wretch on God's earth, not a man that has a worse heart, that breathes in God's air. Did you know me, and the wickedness I am guilty of, and were privy to my secret sins, you would think as well as I that there is no mercy for me, that there is no hope.* Let such a soul consider,

1. *The mercies of God are more and greater than your sins.* Let them never be so great, never so many. Your wickedness does not exceed God's goodness. His goodness is the goodness of a God, and his mercy the mercy of a God, and therefore infinite, without *bonds, limits, or measure.* It is as easy for infinite mercy to forgive many sins as few, and great as small. The sea covers great rocks as well as the smallest sands. If you have a "multitude of sins, God has a multitude of mercies," (Psa. 51:1). If you have "manifold sins," God has "manifold mercies," (Neh. 9:19). If you have "abundantly sinned, God can and will "abundantly pardon," (Isa. 55:7-8). If your sins are sins of "all sorts, of all sizes," God can and will "forgive iniquity, transgression, and sin," (Exod. 34:6-7). Only be willing, heartily willing to leave your sins, only be willing, soundly willing, unfeignedly willing to receive mercy as it is tendered to you, and of Christ the Redeemer as he is offered to you, and the number, the greatness of your sin shall not hinder you from pardon and salvation.

2. *The merits of Christ the Redeemer are fully sufficient to purchase pardon for your sins, were they more and greater*

Chapter 7: Despair

than they be. Do you dare say your sins are more than Christ's sufferings? Or that your debts for which you are in bonds are more than Christ the Surety for poor captives is able to satisfy and pay? *Christ has more pardons than you have sins, more healings than you have wounds*. There is more in Christ to save you than in your sins to condemn you. Your sins are but *pennies* in comparison of the *pounds* that Christ had to pay. Come forward then *poor captive sinner*, approach nearer to your Lord-Redeemer, *come forward*. Why do you go away from him? *Come*, and though you doubt, yet do not despair. If you had not been a sinner, you would have stood in no need of a Savior, and the greater sinner you have been, the greater haste you should make to a Savior. *I think* I hear Christ calling to you, *poor sinner*, why are you thus dismayed at the sight and thoughts of your *iniquities!* Come to me, and I will help you! Why are you so cast down, at the remembrance of what a sinner you have been, and what wickedness you have done? *Come*, I have healing for your wounds, I have bandages for your sores, come to me. I will surely help and heal you. Are you scared by the justice of my Father, come to *me*, rely on *me*, leave your sins, and rely on me, and I will undertake to make your peace with God. And I will get and give you pardon of you sins. *I think* I hear him say, you cry out because you have sinned, and if you had not, there would have been no need of my coming from heaven to earth, there would have been no need of my dying on the cross. *Are you a sinner?* I know you are, and therefore I came on purpose to help you. *Are you a lost sinner?* I know you are, and therefore I came to seek you. *Are you a captive bound in fetters?* I know you are, and therefore I came to ease you, and release you. Only be but heartily willing to receive me for your *prophet, priest, and king*. And consent to the conditions of the gospel. And despond no more as if there were no hope, nor help for you. *Come here*, and see me in my sweat and agony. *Come here* and behold the wounds made in my *side*, my *feet*, my *hands*, my *heart* and all, and these I suffered for such sinners. Look through the wounds made in my side, and see if you cannot see there love in my heart, and pity in my heart to poor returning sinners. What did I suffer for, and what did I bleed and die for, but to help and save poor sinners? Come to me, and I will be your friend. Come to me, believe on me, receive me, and God will be your friend. So then *poor captive soul*, if you are *willing, indeed willing to leave your sins, your fetters and your bonds, to resign your will, your love, your heart to Christ, make him your end, and take him for your Lord-Redeemer*, there is no reason you should despair of pardon and salvation. Do not then let Satan keep you in this bond, from coming to Christ, to be set at liberty.

3. *Your sins and your wickedness are not greater, are not more than all the sins of all the elect of God were that are now in heaven.* And yet mercy has pardoned them, and yet Christ's merits have purchased life and salvation for them, and they are now in possession of it. If you have out-sinned any *one single man*, yet have you committed more, or greater sins than *all the sins of all the millions now in glory*. Put them all together, and yet has God been able and willing to pardon them, and Christ able and willing to save them? If you will repent and believe, as they did you shall be saved as they are! If you will leave your sins and be converted, as they were, do not despair, no, do not doubt, but you shall be happy as they are. Have you sinned more than Adam did, that at one blow wounded and killed so many souls, as never man did, no, nor ever shall again? Have you sinned more than Manasseh, read

Chapter 7: Despair

and judge, (2 Chron. 33:1-14)? Have you sinned more than Paul that was a bloody persecutor of God's people, (1 Tim. 1:13). Have you sinned more than Peter, that did swear and curse that he did not know Jesus Christ? Or more than Mary Magdalene? Or if you *could say*, you have sinned more than all these put together, and thousands of thousands more? You cannot say it. Why then, what is the matter with you, that you sit in your chains lamenting yourself, saying, there is *no hope for me, there is no help, no mercy for me?* What! No hope for a sinner, and a Savior by you? No help, no deliverance for a captive, and the ransom paid, and the Redeemer comes to you, waiting that you would be but willing to receive him for your Lord and Savior, and he is ready to receive you. *Say, O say then*, what did this *tempting* devil mean, one to draw into sin, because it was no great matter that he did tempt me to? And what now does this *accusing* devil mean, that when he has wounded me, would persuade me, there is no healing for me? O my soul! Once this enemy did *befool* you, when he did persuade you, your condition was *so good*, that you did not need to fear, and now shall he *befool* you, to make you think your condition is now *so bad*, that there is no reason why you should hope? *Tell him, O tell him*, that yet his condition is not yours. Though you have sinned, as he has done, yet there is a Savior offered to you, that never was, that never shall be offered to him. O my soul! Satan is bound in this chain of despair himself, and it never can be knocked off. Tell him then, O my enemy, you cannot repent, and therefore cannot hope. You cannot believe, and therefore cannot be saved. Christ did not die for you, but he died for sinful men, that shall have the benefits of his death by believing on him. O I will *now* repent, and by the grace of God I will believe, and while the devil despairs and would hold me from going to Christ, by despairing too. Yet since there is mercy in God and merit in Christ, by which other men have been saved, and this is offered to me, God does call me, and Christ does call me, and the Spirit strives with me to come to Christ, and mercy is promised if I do, and pardon is promised if I do. Why then should I sit here lamenting of my doleful case? Or why do I sit here despairing of mercy? I will arise and go and venture to cast myself on Christ, and trust my soul with him. If I stay here from Christ, I am sure I shall perish. But if I go, it may be I shall live. Did I say it *may* be; O God has declared in his word that if I do repent, and believe, that it shall be, that I shall be saved. Resolve therefore as those four lepers that said to one another, "Why do we sit here until we die. If we say we will enter into the city, then the famine is in the city, and we shall die there. And if we sit still here, we die also. Now therefore come, and let us fall into the hosts of the Syrians. If they save us alive, we shall live. And if they kill us we shall but die," (2 Kings 7:3-4). If you sit still in your natural state, and will not go to Christ, you shall surely die, and if you go to him, you need not say *I can but die*, for if you go, you *shall not die*. So then (though all this be no ground to encourage any to go on in sin, and yet hope for heaven, who were spoken to before, yet) all this is reason of encouragement to those that have already sinned, and are *penitentially grieved* that they have done so, that they should now *despair* as once they did *presume*. And the Lord grant that as you have been convinced and awakened, that you might be no longer kept in bondage by presumption, so now you might go to Christ the Redeemer of captives, and not be kept captives still and perish by despair.

CHAPTER 8: THE 6th AND 7th LINKS – MORALITY AND RELIGIOUS DUTIES

A 6th chain is taking up morality. 7. And resting in religious duties.

Another chain by which many of these captives are bound is *their satisfying themselves with a moral blameless life*. One says, I live peaceably among my neighbors, I defraud no man, I am just in all my dealings, I give to everyone their due. Another says, I am no drunkard, no swearer, no open profaner of Sabbaths, no man can lay anything to my charge, nor say my eye is black. Many sinners rest here, and do persuade themselves their condition is good, and do not think that they are in bondage to the devil, and so do not look out after redemption by Jesus Christ.

Though all this is good in itself, yet it does not argue that your condition is good, because it is not sufficient to salvation, for as much as God requires this and something more, no, much more than this that you may be meet for heaven. Towards the breaking of this bond, *consider,*

1. *Negative holiness is not a ground of hope for future glory, nor a proof of a present good condition.* Negatives in reference to affirmative precepts will damn, but negatives in reference to forbidding precepts will not save. There are commands of God enjoining you to repent, and believe, to pray and to forsake sin. Your *not repenting, not believing* will undo your souls. And there are commands enjoining you not to be drunkards, not to be swearers, not to defraud, nor overreach others in your dealings. Now if you are not *drunkards*, yet if you

are not believers you are still in Satan's bonds. You must not only not do evil, but you must also do that which is good, (Isa. 1:16-17; Matt. 25:42).

2. *If you are of a blameless life, yet you have a corrupt and sinful heart.* If you have been free all your lifelong from every actual sin (as you are not) yet there is sin enough in your heart to sink you to the lowest hell. There is heart adultery, and heart murder, pride of heart, and unbelief in your heart. So that though you say, *fair is your life*, yet God does see, that *foul and filthy is your heart.* And it is not blamelessness of life only, but purity of heart too, that must qualify you for the enjoyment of God, (Matt. 5:8; Heb. 12:14).

Have you wronged no man? What! Nor God neither! Do you give to every man his due? What! And to God too? Your heart is God's due, (Prov. 23:26). Do you give to God your heart, which is his due? Your love and obedience is God's due, (Matt. 22:37). Do you indeed give these to God? Your time and service and religious worship is God's due, (Matt. 4:10). Do you deny these to God, and yet boast that you give to everyone their due? Or do you look on it as an evil, to withhold from man, that which does belong to him, and is it not a greater evil to withhold from God, that which does belong to him? Will you *pay me, and rob God*, and yet hold yourself guiltless? Will you be righteous towards men, and unholy towards God, and yet hold yourself innocent? Where the same God that does command you to live *soberly* towards yourself, and *righteously* towards men, does also charge you to be *holy* towards him, (Titus 2:12). What if you are at peace with all men, if you are not at peace with God? Are you not a captive still? What, if you are in charity with the entire world (as you make your boast) if you have no love to God? Are you not in fetters still? What if you bear no malice in your heart to any man, yet if your heart is full of hatred and enmity to God, has not the devil yet held fast on you? Did you never read Matthew 19:18-20, that you as a moralist said as much as you do say, and yet he remained still in the bonds of his iniquity? Did you never read Luke 18:11, where the Pharisee boasted to God himself, that *he was not as other men are, that he was no extortioner, no adulterer, nor unjust, and yet not being justified was fast bound in the guilt of sin?* A moral man without converting, sanctifying grace is like a *swine* in a fair meadow, that though it is not there wallowing in the mire, yet it is a swine still. O then do not stay here, since there are many now in hell that were not common drunkards, swearers, nor profane debauched persons, do not let Satan keep you any longer bound in your captive state with this bond of your applauded moral conversation.

    7. Another chain with which some captives are bound is their *resting in religious and holy duties*. These go a step higher than the former, and yet are as fast bound as others are, and faster too. For when many gross sinners are delivered from captivity, and their bonds are broke, hypocrites are fast entangled with chains of their own making. Publicans and harlots enter into the kingdom of God, when hypocrites are shut out, (Matt. 21:31). As Paul compared himself with others, "Are they Hebrews? So am I. Are they Israelites? So am I. Are they the seed of Abraham? So am I. Are they ministers of Christ? I am more in labors more abundant, in stripes above measure, in prisons more frequent, in deaths often," (2 Cor. 11:22). So hypocrites comparing themselves with those that are set at liberty by Christ in respect of *all external duties*, and *common gifts*, conceiting that therefore they are free to, are the faster bound. Are God's freemen much in prayer? So am I, says the

hypocrite. Are they frequent in hearing? So am I. Are they admitted to all ordinances, and received into church fellowship by the godly, strict, and careful ministers of Christ? So am I. Do they talk and discourse of God, and Christ, and heaven? So do I, and more than many of them do. Do they suffer for religion, and have been in bonds and prisons for religious worshiping of God? So have I.

These are strong bonds, and the more they pray and hear, the stronger are their bonds, while they are praying and hearing, the devil is *binding* these captive hypocrites so much the faster, and this is their misery more especially, that these *chains* which are made for their *close imprisonment*, they do look on as *chains of ornament*, and do glory in them. For the breaking of this bond, *consider,*

1. *The external performance of religious duties has been done by many now in hell.* Some of the *now* damned souls, when in their bodies were often present at sermons as well as you, and often on their knees as well as you. And yet were then in the bonds of sin, and you also may yet be, and are now in chains in utter darkness, which God in mercy grant that you may never be. *Outward duties* may be done to God, when there is *inward prevailing love* to self, to sin, and to the world. It is not so much the *matter* as the *manner* of your duties, that argues your freedom from captivity, not *what* you do, as *from what principle*, and *for what end* you do, as *from what principle*, and *for what end* you do them that does distinguish the devil's captives from the Lord's freemen. Christ plainly tells you that not everyone that makes a profession of religion shall be delivered from the prison of hell, (Matt. 7:21-23). And that the children of the kingdom shall be cast into outer darkness, (Matt. 8:12). Know therefore that though you should hear ten

thousand sermons, and make as many prayers, yet *without an inward real change* by converting grace above all, and choose and prize Christ before all, that you may not be released from captivity for the present, nor saved hereafter.

    2. *There is no certain judgment that can be made of your spiritual slavery or freedom by the thoughts that others have of you.* Men judge *charitably*, but God judges *certainly*. Men judge your *hearts* by your *actions*, but God judges your *actions by your hearts*. You might be admitted among the purest congregation, and yet not be admitted into heaven. If Christ himself were on the earth you might be an hearer of Christ, and yet a captive to the devil. Christ tells you as much, (Luke 13:26-28). And I pray you, what is it to be applauded or approved by men, and to be condemned by God? You are not to stand or fall, to be damned or saved by what men think of you, but by what God knows of you. Remember Judas, that carried himself so among others, that the rest of the disciples did rather suspect themselves rather than him, saying, "Lord, is it I?", and another "Is it I?" when Christ told them, one of them should betray him. Remember him, and beware, that as others are bound captives with the bonds of open and *visible iniquity*, that you do not remain bound with the bonds of hidden and secret hypocrisy.

CHAPTER 9:
THE 8th, 9th AND 10th LINKS

Containing the 8th, 9th, and 10th chains or bonds of these captives.

Another chain by which some are held captive is *the example of others.* And these are either the examples (1) of those that *lived formerly,* or (2) those that are *now alive.* And one says, *I am of the same religion as my forefathers were. My father, and my father's father were of this way, and who will say our forefathers were not redeemed, nor are saved? Who will say that our forefathers died captives and are gone down to hell? Will any zealous preacher of them all condemn our forefathers? And should we be wiser than our forefathers?* Besides, if we look to this present age, another says, *the greatest part of the world live as I do, or worse. And if my condition is not good, God helps many others. Will God send such multitudes to hell? And if I am damned, woe be to thousands. It will be others' case as well as mine.* Both of these ways are persons held in their captivity. Towards breaking then of this bond and cutting off this chain, consider in answer to the first.

1. *We have nothing to do to pass any sentence on your forefathers.* They are out of the reach of our preaching and exhortations. We leave them to the righteous judgment of God, who has disposed of them *before this day* to the places where they must be forever. And God does not send us to tell you, where your forefathers are gone. Our message is to you that are yet alive, and our business and employment is to tell you of your sin and misery, and to call you to repentance, and to acquaint you with the conditions of peace to be made between God and you. To tell you, what *you* must be, and what *you* must do to escape the damnation of hell, and to be partakers of the

redemption which Christ has purchased for poor captive sinners.

2. *You might be of the same profession of religion as your forefathers were, and they might be saved, and yet you might be damned.* They might be redeemed and delivered, and yet you still remain captives. Your forefathers professed faith in Christ, prayed to God, and performed religious duties to God, as you profess to do. And yet if they did these things sincerely, and you hypocritically, they in reality and you in show, their souls are now in glory and at rest, where your souls notwithstanding may never be. Many of the same age make the same profession, and yet some are good, and some are bad. Some are made free, and some continue captives. As the five foolish virgins made the same profession as the wise, (Matt. 25:1-13), and Judas, as the rest of the disciples. And yet the one was captivated, while the others were redeemed. And so it may be with persons that live and profess in several ages.

3. *But why should you content yourselves in being such as your forefathers were?* Though I do not, dare not, will not say that they are damned. Yet are you *so sure* that they are saved? Are you all sure, that all your forefathers believed, and repented, that they were all sanctified and saved? *If so*, surely *that age was better than this*, and it would have been better to have lived then than now. But if they did not believe, did not repent, would you then go to the place where they are now? Or would it be any ease to your pain to meet any of your forefathers there? Your wisest, fastest course is not to say, we will live as our forefathers did, but as God in his word does command and direct you to do.

4. *But why might you not be wiser and better than your forefathers were?* Were they perfect in wisdom and goodness?

If they were not wise indeed for heaven and their souls, and if they were not good indeed, you must be wiser and better than they were, or you shall not be saved. If they were truly wise and good, it was their burden and their grief that they were no wiser, and no better, and why should that be a fault in you to be wiser than they were, which they complained of as a fault in themselves that they were no wiser, and no better than they were?

Besides, would you not be *richer* than your forefathers were? And *greater* and *more honorable* in the world if possibly you can? Do you not labor for greater estates than they had, had they much or had they little? Had they little, would you not have much? Had they much, would you not have more? If you would be richer and greater, why may you not endeavor to be wiser, and to be better than they were?

5. *What if some of your forefathers should come from the dead, and tell you they were mistaken, and deceived, and are damned, and have been in hell ever since they died?* Would you think yourselves concerned then to be wiser and to be better than they were? If your father or your father's father should come to any of you, and say, "O! Do not slight Christ as we did, do not, our poor posterity, remain in a natural state as we did, and are now suffering the wrath of God, and the vengeance of eternal flames. O! Do not follow our *example*, nor lead your lives *as we did*, and neglect to worship God in your families, or do it half-heartedly, carelessly and negligently *as we did*, lest you come to the same place of torment, as we are condemned into, and must be in forever. Take *the Scripture for your rule, and not our example*. Do not follow us, O do not follow us in sin, in careless neglect of God and Christ, lest you follow us to hell and to damnation too. If you content

yourselves to live and die as we did, captives to the devil, and your children after you, content themselves to follow and to imitate you, as you do to imitate and to follow us, the race that did descend from us will be damned from one generation to another." Would you after such warning as this plead your forefathers' examples no more? Do not then let the devil lead you any longer captives by this bond of their example, as if this were more binding than the commands of God.

For the breaking of the other piece of this cord by which the devil binds his captives. The examples of those that live in the same age, the most live as I do. Will God damn such multitudes? If it goes ill with me, God help many others. *Consider,*

1. *The most are not the best.* The greatest number is of the bad sort of men. Christ's flock is but little, (Luke 12:32), while the devil has great droves, (Matt. 7:13-14). If you will follow the multitude, they will lead you to a place of sorrow, (Exod. 23:2).

2. *At the Day of Judgment will be no escaping in a crowd.* You shall not speed the better because multitudes sin as well as you. If thousands continue captives to the devil, they shall all be damned? God will damn millions of men, rather than falsify his word, if men sin in companies, they shall suffer in companies.

3. *That multitudes are carried captives to hell, will not make your chains lighter, nor your pains easier.* When you are in hell, to lie there and look round about you, and see multitudes there besides yourself, there will be no mitigation of your torments. Multitudes sinning does not lessen your sin, and multitudes being damned will not lessen your damnation. God has enough wrath for you and them. Though he pours out

more on millions than they can bear, yet he has enough to inflict on you, and more than you can endure. Would you be in Turkish slavery, because more are there besides yourself. Seriously ponder this, and do not let Satan keep you captive to bear others' company.

9. Another chain by which these captives are kept in their bondage state, is their *purposing hereafter to repent and forsake their sins.* In your *childhood* you did purpose to repent when you should come to *man's estate.* Then, when you should be *old,* and now, when you come to be *sick and die,* and thus from your birth to your death, you continue a captive, and by these delaying purposes die so. To break this bond, *consider,*

1. *Who was it that did assure you that you shall certainly live to that time in which you purpose to repent?* Did God or man? Man cannot. God does not tell sinners how long they shall live. How do you come to have this knowledge above others? No, I have not. No? What? And yet purpose to repent, and shake off the devil's bonds hereafter, when your body might be in your grave, and your soul in hell before that time may come? Where will your repentance be then? Are you not as young as you once were, and will you go down into the pit of grave and hell too? Go and view the burial places of the dead, measure and see if there is no grave as short as you are, and many graves of infants there. You are here today and might be in eternity tomorrow. Now alive, tomorrow may be dead. All flesh is compared to grass, (Isa. 40:6-8; Matt. 6:30), to a vapor, (James 4:13-15). Was he not a fool that reckoned he had many years to live, (Luke 12:19-20)? When you go to bed, how do you know that you will rise anymore? When you fall asleep that you shall awake, until the trumpet sound, and the call is, *Arise you dead, and come to judgment?*

Chapter 9: The 8th, 9th and 10th Links

2. *How do you know that when you shall be sick, that you shall have the use of your reason and understanding?* If not, where is your repentance then? Have you not often seen sick persons to be deprived of their understanding? Not capable of asking or receiving of counsel and advice?

3. *Is repentance in your own power?* Or can you repent when you wish? Can you? The more you are to blame, the more is your sin and shame that you do not now repent. Can you not? The more is your folly, to put it off as though you could. No, the longer you continue in your sin, the harder your heart will be, and the harder your heart is, the harder work it will be for you to break it, (Jer. 13:23).

4. *Do you read of any more than one man that did repent at last, at a dying hour in all the word of God?* Is there any spoken of for this besides the thief on the cross? If you have but this one single example, why will you venture your eternal state on this?

5. *Do you not do your purposing to repent and leave the service of Satan and sin hereafter, imply a present resolution that yet you are resolved to go on in sin?* And is it not more wickedness to resolve to be a servant to the devil and your lusts until you are sick or old, than goodness in you, to purpose then to be a servant of God? When you will have neither time nor strength to do him any service, no, nor heart either. Judge if this is reasonable, and if not, do not let Satan keep you captive by this any longer.

6. *Is it fit then that you should give the first of your time and strength to Satan rather than to God?* Is it not wickedness to say I will first serve the devil, and after him God? Shall God have the devil's leavings? Will you give the devil the best of your time and God the dregs?

7. Does God not require your present turning and present repentance, (Heb. 4:7; Eccl. 12:1)?

8. If you are poor, would you not be rich presently? And if in pain, would you not have present ease? And are not God, Christ and grace more desirable?

9. If you had drunk a cup of poison, would you not have a present remedy to save your lives?

10. Might not God give you up to spiritual judgments, to hardness of heart, and to the reigning power of sin, and say be filthy still, (Rev. 22:11), and say his Spirit shall strive no longer with you, (Gen. 6:3).

10. Another chain that keeps them fast indeed is *their unbelief*, a willful refusing to receive of Christ, the only Lord-Redeemer as he is offered to them in the gospel. This is the chain that binds the guilt of all other sins on their souls. To break this bond, *consider*,

1. *There is no other Redeemer than Christ, (Acts 4:12).* If you will not own him, nor submit to him, you must perish in your bonds and die without redemption. For other sins, the wrath of God comes on men, (Col. 3:5-6). But by reason of unbelief the wrath of God *abides* on them, (John 3:36), and they abide in their captivity.

2. *This is the greatest folly.* Is it not folly to prefer bonds before liberty? Especially when you might come out free, freely, without any price paid down by you, but by the ransom which the Redeemer has already given to God, and the benefit offered to you. But you thrust the Redeemer from you, as the *Israelites* did Moses that came to bring them out of bondage, (Acts 7:27).

3. *This is the highest ingratitude*, that the Son of God should be bound, that you may not be forever bound. He condemned, that you may be acquitted. He suffered that you

Chapter 9: The 8ᵗʰ, 9ᵗʰ and 10ᵗʰ Links

may be saved, and offers to you the benefit of his redemption, and calls and commands and waits for your response. But you prefer the world and sin before him, and would rather keep your sins with *chains of bondage* than receive him for Lord and Savior with a *crown of glory*. You see by this time what are the bonds with which Satan has held you bound so long. O now beg that they may be broken? If not, consider further that which follows.

CHAPTER 10: CAPTIVITY BY SATAN

Showing that the captivity of sinners by Satan, is worse than the captivity of men in corporal slavery.

Having set before you the resemblance of sinners to captives, and several of the chains by which they are bound in this captivity, I shall next proceed to show you in which the condition of these captives is far worse than any captives under the sun besides. And I beg you in *the fear of God*, seriously weigh your danger, and in good sadness consider your misery before you are past remedy, recovery, and redemption. If all I have already said be forgotten, and has been lighted by you. Yet do not stop your ears, stiffen your necks, and harden your hearts against what shall be further propounded to you to awaken your consciences. In respect of *civil liberty* you are all freeborn, and many of you are *free citizens*. But yet being Satan's captives, and sin's bondmen, your case is *deplorable*. Though yet through mercy tendered to you, and waiting to this day on you, it is not *deplorable*. If it should move compassion in us to hear of any carried captive by a cruel enemy, as Jeremiah's eyes were filled with tears, and his heart with sorrow, when he did consider the captive state of God's people, "But if you will not hear it, my soul shall weep in secret places for your pride, and my eyes shall weep sore, and run down with tears, because the Lord's flock is carried away captive," (Jer. 13:17). "Hear, I pray you, all people, and behold my sorrow. My virgins and my young men are gone into captivity," (Lam. 1:18). Much more should it be lamented with abundant tears and sorrow of heart that sinners are captivated by the devil, by how much this captivity is sorer than any other, as appears by these particulars following.

1. *It is spiritual bondage, and the captivity of the soul.* If a man is a slave to men, they have power only over his body and outward man, and his soul may be free. The nobler the subject is, the more grievous is the bondage. Things that concern the soul, if good, they are the best, as *promises* of blessings to the soul are the best promises, and *mercies* for the soul are the best mercies. So if things that concern the soul are bad, they are the worst. *Threatenings* against the soul are the sorest threatenings, and punishments on the soul are the sorest and the heaviest punishments. And the loss of the soul is the greatest loss, "What does it profit a man if he gains the whole world and loses his own soul? Or what shall a man give in exchange for his soul?" (Matt. 16:26). It were better to have the body fettered with as many chains as it could carry, if the soul is free, than to have the body be at liberty to go up and down where you will, if the body be in bondage to Satan and to sin. *Sinner*, it is your soul, your *only, precious, and immortal soul* that is in chains. And you are at rest, eat, drink, and sleep with so much peace while your soul is carried captive? Can you be so merry and so jovial with fetters on your soul? Can you buy and sell and trade with so much earnestness after worldly gain, while Satan has possession of your soul? If your lands were mortgaged, would you not be careful to redeem them? If your jewels were in pawn, would you not be mindful to have them to be restored to you? What! Do you prize and value a few acres of land, the very earth you tread on, above your soul? Are a thousand jewels better than this one only jewel of your soul? Would you not be moved with pity to see malefactors (whose time of execution is approaching) card and dice, carouse and drink, and sing with chains rattling at their heels? And do you not have pity for yourself, and no compassion for yourself,

whose time of death and execution draws nigh, and will quickly come, and yet can be so light-hearted, when the devil has your soul in worse than iron fetters? *Does not this lightness of your heart plainly prove the hardness of your heart?* Remember, you had better have your body possessed by a thousand devils, or torn by a thousand devils into a thousand pieces, than to have your precious soul led captive by the devil, and held his prisoner by the reigning power of any one lust whatsoever. Will you think of this, it is your soul that is a captive, and in bonds?

    2. This captivity and bondage to Satan and to sin, is worse than any other, in that *these captives are not sensible of their thralldom*, do not lament themselves, nor bewail their own condition, though it is so bad, so very bad. The children of Israel did groan and sigh by reason of their bondage, (Exod. 2:22). When Manasseh was bound with fetters, and carried captive to Babylon, he was sensible of the fetters on his body, that had before no sense of the bonds of sin, with which he was held in bondage by the devil. And how do poor captives sigh and groan under Turkish slavery, and bitterly lament because of the hard usage they are under? And how do many prisoners grieve and take on that they did that for which they are in irons? Do men need to spend many hours, and make many long orations, to convince a captive among the Turks of the sadness of his condition there? But how many hours must a minister spend in studying and in preaching before these captives can be brought to a sense of their own woeful and miserable condition? Before he can convince them that indeed they are in this captivity? It is indeed but here and there one among a multitude that do see it, believe it, and bewail it. Who is witness of your groans, and of your tears? When did you

complain to God or man of the fetters and the bonds of sin that have been so long on your souls? When did you retire to your closet, and there lament your woeful case. Is not this a dreadful case to be near to hell, and not to see it? To be near damnation, and not to fear it? To be led by the devil in the chains of sin, to a place of torment, and to be not at all sensible where you are going? Shall nothing but the flames of hell convince you of your bondage? Will you not believe that the devil is leading you to hell until you see and find and feel that you are there? Will you not yield that you are of the number of Satan's captives on earth, until he brings you to the lake of burning brimstone, and look round about you, and then to your eternal sorrow see that you are one of the number of the captive souls in hell? This makes your captivity the sorer, and your bonds the stronger, that you are not sensible of your bondage.

3. So does this too, that *you are a voluntary bond-slave to Satan and to sin.* You are the devil's servant, and are willing to be so. In bondage, and are willing to remain in it. *You might have liberty, but you will not.* You are like the servant that plainly said, I love my master, I will not go out free, and would rather have his ears bored through with an awl, and serve him forever, than be made free, (Exod. 21:5-6). Slaves in Turkey are there against their wills, it is not a matter of their choice. They are captives, but they are not willing captives. They do not love their fetters, nor their chains, nor the work and service that they are there put to, but you are in captivity to Satan, and you love to have it so. You drudge in his service, and do love to do it. But what will you do in the end thereof? (Jer. 5:31). Others are by power and force taken and continued captives, but you do voluntarily yield yourself to be a slave. For Satan could not have taken men captive, nor held them in there, without their

own consent. Like Ahab, you do sell yourself for a slave, (1 Kings 21:20). And what do you sell yourself, your soul, a captive for? For a little profit, and for a little short and momentary pleasure? That you might gratify your lust, for a while, and please your palate and your flesh for a while, you are content to be a slave forever. When a man is taken captive, *yet his will is not taken.* When his body is fettered, yet his will is not overcome. He has a will to resist still, if he had but power. He has a will to have his chains off, though he cannot. And a will to escape, and be set at liberty, though there is none to lay down a ransom for him. But the devil's captives have no will to be delivered or freed from their bondage, though there is a ransom paid, and the benefit of it be offered to them.

  4. *It is a plenary and full captivity.* The entire sinner is in bondage, not only the will, but all the powers and affections of the soul, so that there is nothing free in him. If a man is in bondage to men, his thoughts might be free, and his affections might be free, free to love God, free to delight in God, free to desire after God. But Satan's captives have no freedom to anything that is spiritually good and pleasing to God. Therefore, this is a sore bondage.

  5. *These captives are children of the wrath of God.* Where others that are captives to men might be children of the love of God as they love and delight in God when they are in chains, so God may love and delight in them. If a man's outward condition is never so bad, yet he might comfort himself with the thoughts of God's love to him. *Though I am in prison, yet God loves me, and though I am in chains, yet God loves me.* But the devil's captives do not love God, nor are beloved by him. God has had a love of *goodwill* to many of these captives, a love of purpose to do them good in delivering them from their

bonds. But a love of *complacency and delight* so that God should take pleasure in you while you are voluntarily and totally the devil's slaves and servants, there is not in God towards you. O did you but know the wrath of God, the fury of the Lord, what it is, how great, how intolerable. Could you please yourselves in that condition in which you are the objects of his wrath? As there is no love like the love of God, so there is no wrath like the wrath of God. Therefore, that condition (be it what it will) is not so bad in which you may be the object of God's love, as that condition is in which you are and must be the objects of his wrath.

6. *Death does not deliver Satan's captives from their thralldom and their bondage, but straightens their bonds and strengthens their chains, and puts them into an impossibility of redemption forever.* If a slave is no way delivered while he lives, yet he is freed when he dies. Death will bring him a release, and give him a discharge. "There the wicked cease from troubling, and there the weary are at rest. There the prisoners rest together, they do not hear the voice of the oppressor. The small and great are there, and the servant is free from his master," (Job 3:17-19). When the king of Babylon had taken Zedekiah captive, and bound him in fetters, he put him in prison until the day of his death, and then he was his prisoner no longer, (Jer. 52:12). But these are captives until *they die,* and which is worse, are captives *after death.* The others might say and comfort themselves by which, *Well, this is hard, but it is not lasting. This is bitter, but it will have an end.* Though it lasts as long as life shall last, yet death will come, and then we shall be released. But these may say, *It is bad while we live, and it will be worse when we die.* If we are not delivered while we

live, death will not, death cannot deliver us. Therefore, this is worse than any other bondage.

7. *A worse and more dreadful prison is prepared for the devil's captives than any slaves on earth can be cast into.* Hell is the prison appointed and prepared for all captives that are not made free by Christ, (1 Peter 3:19). Several things make this prison worse than any other.

1. The prison prepared for these captives is a *closed prison.* Now you are like prisoners that sometimes might walk abroad with their keeper with them. Now you are a *prisoner at large,* that walks up and down, though in your chains of sin and guilt, and the devil your keeper does attend and watch you wherever you go. If you come to a sermon, your keeper comes with you, to prevent your breaking loose, and when you go from the sermon, to tempt you to return to your course of sin again. But hereafter you shall be a *close prisoner,* not suffered to step out forever. And so closed shall you be kept that none shall come at you, to visit or to comfort you. It is an alleviation of a prisoner's grief, though he does not have liberty to go out and see his friends. Yet his friends might come and see and visit him. But neither shall be allowed to you when once you are close prisoners in hell. Your friends on earth will not be desirous of your company, or your visits after death, if you had the liberty to come forth. Such visits of damned souls would be a burden, and disquietment, and a terror to the living. That would then rather wish that you were confined to your prison than to be permitted to come forth to disturb them by your visits. Neither shall any be suffered to come and comfort you, if they would. And indeed, none would be desirous, nor venture so far to come to hell to comfort you, if they might. Though the rich man desired that Lazarus might come and comfort him

with one drop of water, it would not be granted to him, for he was a close prisoner, (Luke 16:24-25). Besides, there is a great gulf fixed between them and the saints above, that there is no passing from the one place to the other, (Luke 16:26).

2. *It is a dark prison*, a very dungeon, a place of utter darkness, a place where there is thickness and blackness of darkness forever, (Matt. 25:30; Jude 13). Darkness adds to the discomfort of the condition they must be in, in that prison forever. It was an amazing judgment on the Egyptians, to be under *thick darkness* for three days, (Exod. 10:22-23). What a dreadful dungeon this world would be without the light of sun, moon, stars, or candle, though you were not in pain, nor want of further outward enjoyments, yet it would be no desirable place to continue in. O then, what will the sadness, frights, and fears be of these captives forever, that shall be in pain, in torment, and in darkness forever? If a man were to live all his days in a place, to have rich provisions to feed on, and beds of down to lodge on, but yet to be always in the dark, would be a great affliction to him. O then, what will it be to live in pain and darkness too? To lie and roll and tumble in a bed of flames, in a lake of brimstone, and in darkness too? To be among devils, and this in darkness too? And must not that be a place of darkness forever, where the light of God's countenance shall not shine on the prisoners there forever?

3. *It is a filthy prison*, full of noisome stenches, and unsavory smells. Prisons are filthy places, very offensive to the nostrils, but the stench of the brimstone shall be more troublesome to the prisoners there than the most stinking dungeon to any on earth.

4. *It is a strong prison*. As it is so close that none can come to them to comfort them, so it is so strong that not a

prisoner shall escape, or break through, or get out to all eternity. If once these prison doors are shut, and if Christ that has the keys of death and hell does once put you in, and *turn the key on you*, there is no opening them forever. Now you are bound in chains of your own making, even of your sins. But hereafter you shall be bound in chains of God's making. And there are four bars or bolts on the prison gates of hell that the prisoners shall be filled with despair of ever coming forth.

1. These prison gates shall be made fast and strong forever *by the counsel and decree of God*. God has ordained that the imprisonment of those captives that die before they are made free shall be eternal. It is the unalterable will of God that they shall lie in chains forever. God's purpose must be changed before their chains can be broken, or the prisoners delivered. But God is a God that does not change, he will always be in the same mind, and his will shall be the same forever. Therefore, the prisoners must abide by it forever.

2. These prison gates shall be made fast and strong *by the justice of God*. Justice shall keep the prison door, that not a prisoner shall come forth until he has made satisfaction for his sin, until he has paid his debts to the uttermost farthing, and that will never be. When the prisoner has been there a thousand years, and should beg, and pray, *Lord, I have been here a thousand years, it is a long time, a long time. O I think it is a long time since the day I came into this place. My time of sinning seemed short, and it was indeed but short, but my time of suffering seems long. It is indeed exceedingly long. Now therefore, Lord, let me come forth.* No, says justice, yet I am not satisfied. And when the other thousand years are past, and the prisoner should again petition for his liberty, the same answer will be returned. No, says justice, for yet I am not satisfied, and

Chapter 10: Captivity by Satan

until that is done, you must abide in prison. *Must I Lord? Then there is no hope.*

3. These prison gates shall be made fast on the prisoners *by the truth of God.* God has told you in his word, that this fire burns forever, and that the sinner that is not sanctified shall be cast into it, to lodge there forever. The truth of God is eternal truth, and so long as the word of God abides true, so long shall these captives continue in this prison.

4. These prison gates shall be made fast and strong *by the power of God.* There shall be no getting out by force, nor by any opposition that they can make. The same power that sent them there shall keep them that they shall neither die in this prison, nor escape out of it. If then the gates of this prison are fastened by the *unchangeable decree of God,* by the *justice, truth, and power* of God, the prisoners might set their hearts at rest, or rather shall never be at rest, because they shall never come forth from prison.

5. This prison is far worse than any other prison, *because of the company that is there.* And yet in many prisons there is a very wicked crew of swearing, cursing, and cursed company. If a godly man were in some prison among such company, the company would be a great affliction to him than the prison. But if the company of devils, and souls hating and blaspheming God are wicked company, this shall be found in hell, *all bad, not one good among the millions that are there.* As in heaven, *all good, not one bad among the thousands that are there.* Here these captives sin together, and they shall be in prison all together, one cursing and crying out against another, that ever they were acquainted with them on earth. No, then the devil and his slaves shall be in prison together, the

conqueror and the conquered both cast into a lake of brimstone, (Matt. 25:41).

6. *The remembrance of the facts for which these captives shall be cast into this prison will make it worse than any other.* To remember, here we are for obeying the devil rather than God, for hearkening to the temptations of the devil, when we stopped our ears against all the cries, and calls, and counsels of God. Had we but hearkened to the voice of mercy, to the entreaties of Christ, or to the exhortations of his ministers, we would have now been free from this torment and this pain. Had we served God as diligently, daily, and faithfully as we served the devil, we would have now been in a better place, and we should now have had a better reward. O, *why are we damned for our pleasing of our flesh to the displeasing of God?* Do we suffer eternal pains for our folly, in preferring the short pleasures and profits of the world before God, the greatest and chiefest good! For the pleasing of my palate! *This is the fruit of my drinking bouts!* The wine in the glass was not so sweet as the wrath of God in this cup is bitter, which I have been a thousand years a drinking off, but cannot drink it off, but cannot drink it down, but cannot drink it up. O, better I had had so much scalding lead poured down my throat, than those pleasant cups for which I am now in greatest pain. The thoughts of what they shall be in prison for will make the prison more unpleasant.

7. *The remembrance of a price and ransom that was given for captives, and the benefit thereof often tendered to them will make this prison still the more intolerable.* There and then to remember, the Son of God came down from heaven, and did give himself, his blood, his soul, to redeem sinners out of bondage, and this was tendered to me, says one, and to me, says

another, but I like an accursed and unthankful wretch slighted and refused it, says one. And I like a miserable Caitiff preferred my sins and lusts before the Redeemer, says another. We were often warned of this place, and often asked and entreated to receive Christ, and deliverance by him. There was a time that ministers in the name of God came to us Sabbath after Sabbath, and in his name offered liberty to us. How often did they ask us to be willing to leave our bonds, how earnestly did they beg that we would be but willing to have our fetters knocked off, and if we had been but willing, it should have been done. But that time is past, those seasons are gone, and here we lie bound in fetters forever. O time, time, where have you fled? Can it not be recalled, can it not be recalled? O no, no, it cannot be recalled. And those offers shall never be repeated, but to our greater aggravation, by the gnawing worm.

CHAPTER 11: FREEDOM IN CHRIST

Showing what freedom captives set free by Christ enjoy and hope for.

Doctrine 2. The second general head containing the glad tidings to these miserable captives is that there is liberty to be had by Christ. Or, that it is by Christ and Christ alone that poor captive sinners are delivered and set at liberty. Had it not been for Christ, we would have perished in our bonds, and remained in perpetual slavery while we had lived, and been forever bound in chains of darkness, when we die, (Isa. 59:20, applied to Christ; Rom. 11:26; Acts 4:12; John 8:36).

Man might be considered in a fourfold state.

1. In his first condition *as created by God.* Then man was a free man, bondage came in by sin. When man sinned he lost his freedom. And in this estate there was a threefold liberty that man had.

1. *Man was free from sin.* Not the least spot or stain by creation in this pure nature of man. He was then free from pride, and free from the inordinate love of the world, and from everything offensive and displeasing to God, "God made man upright," (Eccl. 7:29). The uprightness of a man renewed by sanctifying grace denotes the sincerity of his heart, though there is sin inherent in him. So Job was an upright man, (Job 1:1). But the uprightness of man at first created by God denotes the perfect image of God in the presence of that which was good, and absence of all sin, (Gen. 1:26-27).

2. Man had a freedom or *liberty of will*, to will and to do what God required from him.

3. *A freedom from all misery*, calamity and punishment. Man had then a freedom from sickness, from sorrow and from

affliction and death, for all these are the fruits of sin. Man had never been in bondage to these, if he had not become a bond-slave to Satan and to sin. And *in this state man had no need of a Redeemer*, because he was not then a captive.

2. Man might be considered in a state of corruption, and so his condition is quite contrary to what it was in his first estate. As before he was free, so now he is a slave, before at liberty, but now in bondage. And this bondage is opposite to the former threefold liberty.

1. In man there is now a bondage to sin, in slavery to his own lusts and to his own vile affections, that there is no part in him free from sin. His *understanding* is not free from ignorance, darkness and error, his *will* is not free from obstinacy and rebellion, his *affections* are not free from disorder and confusion, hating what he should love, and loving what he should hate, shunning what he should desire, and desiring what he should shun, rejoicing in that which should be the matter, cause and reason of his sorrow, and grief, and grieving and being weary of that which should be a matter of his delight and joy. This is man's sinful bondage.

2. *The very will of man is enthralled.* That though man has a liberty of will as to natural actions and to civil actions, and to outward spiritual actions, he can come and hear if he wills, he can set on the outward duty of prayer if he wills. He can read the word of God, if he wills, yet he has no liberty of will to supernatural actions without the grace of God, as to believe on Christ, to love God above all. Man must have a will as well as a power from God to do these things. "It is God that gives us to will and to do of his own good pleasures," (Phil. 2:13). And this is a sore bondage, though a natural man does not feel it, and is not sensible of it.

3. *In bondage by reason of punishment*, being liable to all the curses, plagues, and punishments threatened for sin in the word of God, both in this life and that which is to come, to sickness, and sorrows, to pain and griefs, to death at last, and to hell and damnation after death. And *in this estate man needs a Redeemer, and a ransom*, and is utterly and eternally undone if he is not delivered from this bondage.

3. Man might be considered *in a state of grace* as recovered by Christ, as renewed and restored by the Spirit of God. For God does not suffer all men to remain in their bondage, and those that are redeemed and recovered must not ascribe this to their own free will but to the free grace of God And in *this estate man is made partaker in part of the fruits of redemption by Christ.*

4. Man might be considered *in a state of glory*. And there the saints are all free, and altogether free, they have perfect liberty from sin, from sorrow, from temptations to sin, from all inclination to sin, from a possibility of sinning. And *in this estate the saints do fully and eternally enjoy the fruits of Christ's redemption, and of his giving of himself a ransom for them.*

Question 1. *What is it that we do not have liberty from by Christ the Redeemer?* There are many things that Christ did not come to purchase or proclaim liberty from while we are in this life.

1. None of God's elect are freed by Christ *from being born in original sin*. We are not born free, but are made free. Even those that are descended from freemen in Christ are by birth in spiritual bondage. For grace does not come by blood, but by the will of God, (John 1:13). No man since the fall, except

Christ the Redeemer, has been free from this sinful contagion that has infected all mankind, (Rom. 5:12, 17-18).

2. Christ does not free us in this world *from the indwelling of sin*. Christ does free all believers from the *reigning* power of sin, (Rom. 6:14), but not from the *conflicting* power of sin, no, nor altogether from the *captivating* power of sin. The Lord's freemen might sometimes be overpowered with a temptation, and with a corruption, and in a particular combat be carried captive, (Rom. 7:23). Nor does Christ free us at all from the *indwelling* of sin. As God did not presently free the people of Israel from the nations that vexed them, nor drove them out at once, but by degrees, he left some of them to prove them and to humble them, (Exod. 23:28-29). So all God's redeemed and free servants do still experience the remainders of sin and corruption, and do complain thereof and cry out because of it, (Rom. 7:24). There are still relics of pride, and unbelief, and hardness of heart. So we are not free from distracting thoughts in holy duties, nor from all dullness of affection, and deadness of heart in the service of God. This is reserved for the state of glorious freedom in the life to come, when we shall be and live in the immediate presence of the blessed God above, and shall live in the beholding of him immediately that has redeemed us from our captivity and bondage.

3. Christ has not freed us *from the service of God*, but rather does engage us to it. Wicked men judge this to be liberty to live as they wish, and to walk and act as they please, in gratifying their lusts and pleasing of the flesh. *This is not liberty but licentiousness*. This indeed is the bondage that Christ came to deliver us from. O how the blind world is mistaken, when they take their very bondage for their liberty!

The strictest service of God is the greatest liberty, (Psa. 119:45). It is not a liberty from duty, but from sin and misery that Christ came to purchase and proclaim, (Luke 1:74-75; 1 Peter 2:16; Rom. 6:18). The most under the gospel do live in the constant omission of duty, and commission of sin, as if Christ came to give them liberty to do so, which yet they might have done if Christ had never come.

4. This spiritual freedom by Christ *does not exempt us nor excuse us from the service we owe to men in the places and relations in which God has set us.* Indeed, the Lord's servant must not be the servants of men, so as to love men in that in which they will displease God, (1 Cor. 7:23). But yet one that is the Lord's free man might be in the place of a servant to man, and ought to follow his calling and mind his master's business, and that with greater care and conscience than others do, even to such masters as are the servants of sin, (Eph. 6:5-6; 1 Peter 2:18; Gal. 5:13). And to such matters that are the Lord's freemen, (1 Tim. 6:1-2).

5. *Christ does not free us from afflictions, nor from troubles from men.* Christ has nowhere told us he came to free us from scorns and from reproaches, from prisons, and from tribulations but contrary, (John 16). All God's freemen will be hated by the devil's slaves, and we shall not be freed from them, until we are out of their reach, and that will not be until we get to heaven. Those that have spiritual liberty might lose their civil liberty. As a man might have a civil liberty, but not spiritual, a man might be *free of a city, free of a company,* and yet *not free by Christ.* So a man might be in prison, bound in chains there, and yet be spiritually free. Joseph in the prison, Daniel in the den, Jeremiah in the dungeon, and yet all the Lord's freemen. When Christ calls to many in their bondage to

come to him to be made free, they would indent with Christ that they should enjoy freedom from crosses, and troubles, and sufferings, which because Christ does not free his followers from, they had rather have their freedom from sufferings in their bondage, than sufferings with spiritual freedom.

6. *Christ does not give us freedom from temptations of the devil*, that we should be no more buffeted by that wicked one. Christ himself was not free from temptations from Satan, nor from persecutions from men. Resist the devil, watch and pray against his temptations, for you are not likely to be freed from them, until you get to heaven.

7. *Christ does not free us from the stroke of death*. The Lord's freemen must be bound with death's bonds as well as others. Our souls and bodies are not free from dissolution, your bodies not free from putrefaction. But yet we are freed from the sting of death, and death is not the same to the Lord's freemen as it is to the devil's bondmen.

Question 2. *What is the liberty that we have by Christ?* This shall be managed in speaking to these two particulars. First, as this liberty and freedom is *privative*. Secondly, as it is *positive*, or what we are freed from, and what it is that we are freed to.

1. What it is that believers are freed from by Christ, and these are great and sore evils, and such as would have made us unspeakably and eternally miserable, if Christ had not freed us from them.

1. *Christ has delivered us, and set us free from the power of Satan*, that he has no more rule in us as he formerly had. He did rule in our hearts, (Eph. 2:2). And we did yield voluntary subjection and obedience to him. But Christ has bound this strong man, and spoiled him of his goods, and has dispossessed

him, and turned him out of our hearts, from dwelling, reigning, ruling there, as on a throne. Christ came to do this, (Heb. 2:14-15). He has delivered us from the justice of God, by *price and purchase*. From Satan, by *power* and by a *mighty hand*.

2. *Christ has set us free from sin*. Not for the present, or in this life from the indwelling of sin, as you heard before, but in these two respects:

1. By Christ believers have a *freedom from the guilt of sin*. We are free from the obligation that lays on us to eternal torments. So that now we shall never come into condemnation for our sins. Our many sins are all pardoned, our great and heinous sins are all forgiven, (Rom. 8:1, 33-34). Many might accuse. The devil might accuse, and men might accuse, and conscience might accuse, and the Law might accuse us. But Christ has so freed us that none can condemn. O what a blessed peace of our freedom lies in this! What would you have done, to have answered for your sins? What would you have done to bear the punishment of your sins? Indeed, you could neither answer for yourself, nor yet have borne the wrath of God due to you for your sin. O then see the everlasting obligation laid on you to love this blessed Christ, to prize and value, and esteem this once crucified, and now glorious Christ that has taken off this obligation from you. He has freed you from one obligation, and by it laid on you another. He has freed you from an obligation to eternal condemnation, and has laid on you a strong and lasting obligation to love him and to praise and admire his love and grace to you forever.

2. *Christ has set us free from the dominion of sin*. The sinner was the captive, and sin the Lord and conqueror. But he that is made free by Christ is made the conqueror, and sin the captive. The victory indeed is not yet completed, yet sin is

enthroned. The sinner, when a captive was in chains, but now made free, sin is become bound. Sin was delighted in, but now it is abhorred. Sin was voluntarily yielded to, but now resisted and opposed. Sin was welcomely entertained, but now lamented and bewailed. It was looked on with pleasure and content, but now it is beheld with a sorrowful heart, and with a weeping eye. It is become the burden and the grief that before had the love and complacency of the sinner's heart, it is now prayed against, and watched against, and endeavored against that before was indulged and allowed and provided for, and willingly submitted to. Now says the redeemed sinner, my hard heart is a burden to me. My proud and unbelieving heart is a burden and a grief to me. My vain and worldly heart is a burden, and a trouble, and a sorrow to me. He is freed from the reigning power of sin, (Rom. 6:14).

 7. *Christ has set believers free from the curse of the Law.* The Law has its use under the gospel. By it we come to the "knowledge of sin," (Rom. 3:20; 5:20). By it we are "convinced of our misery" that by sin we have deserved death and damnation, (Rom. 7:10) that we might *see the necessity of Christ*, and hasten the more to him, (Gal. 3:24). It *serves for a rule* to direct us in our walking, and for *a glass* in which we see the imperfection of our duty and obedience, that we might not rest in them, nor trust them for life and salvation. But from the condemning sentence and curse of the law, Christ has made believers free, by being made a curse for them himself, (Gal. 3:10, 13).

 4. *Christ has set believers free from the hurt of death.* The Lord's freemen must die as well as the devil's bondmen. But death will be another thing to a freeman, than it is to a captive. So that which is formidable to a sinner, is desirable to a saint.

Christ has taken away the sting of death, (1 Cor. 15:55), of an enemy is become a friend, and death, that is one of the plagues that befall the devil's captives is become part of the charter of the Lord's freemen, (1 Cor. 3:22).

1. Death to freemen of the Lord is the *utter abolition of their sin*. It shall free them from the very being and indwelling of sin. When the soul shall be separated from the body, all sin, and all corruption shall be separated from the soul. Whereas the devil's bondmen die in their sin, and after death do still retain their hatred to God, their enmity to Christ, and are more confirmed and hardened in it than before.

2. Death to the Lord's freemen *puts an end to all their sorrow and affliction*, to all their troubles and their sufferings. It is God's handkerchief, by which he wipes away all tears from the eyes of his redeemed people, (Rev. 14:13). But at death the sorrow of the devil's captives does begin, or is increased, if they were at ease while they lived, they shall be in pain when they die. If they did roar and sing, while they lived, they shall roar and lament after death. Death takes them from their riches, from their friends, and from their pleasure, and whatever was dear to them in this world's enjoyment, and puts them into a place of pain and torment, a place of utter darkness, where they shall forever weep and howl, and fruitlessly lament their woeful state, and their irrecoverably lost happiness.

3. Death of the Lord's freemen is *the gate to glory, and their passage and entrance into eternal life*. It is the opening of the door to let them into their father's house, a messenger sent by God to fetch them into the presence of their God and Redeemer, to live, and reign, and dwell with him forever, that their freedom here begun might be consummated and perfected

Chapter 11: Freedom in Christ

in heaven. In that very day they die, they are admitted as free citizens of the glorious kingdom of God, (Luke 16:22).

4. Death to the Lord's freemen *shall come in the best time*. All men die in God's time, whenever he appoints. But the redeemed by Christ shall die in the best time, when their work is done, and when God sees it is better for them to die than to live. God takes the best time and fittest season for the removing of his by death out of the world. But the wicked slaves of sin and Satan are cut off in *a bad time, whenever they die*. It is a bad time to them, because whenever it is, they go that day to hell, and to eternal torments. The day of their dissolution is the day of their damnation. And will that not be the saddest day they ever had? *They die before their work is done*. Before they have believed, and before they have repented, and that must be a sad day whenever it comes. Men cut down weeds at any time, but the corn in the best time, in the fittest season, when it is ripe to be carried into the barn.

5. Death, for the Lord's freemen, *has lost its terribleness*. And though all God's redeemed are not actually and totally freed from the fears of death, but sometimes kept in bondage through the fears of death, yet they have grounds and reasons why they might not fear it. But the devil's captives always have cause and reason to be terribly afraid of death. And if they are not, it arises from the blindness of their minds, and the hardness of their hearts. *It is a wonder that men should be as near to hell as to the grave, and yet not be afraid to die. It is a wonder that men should be as near to an endless miserable life, as they are to the end of this short uncertain life, and yet their fears should not prevent their sleeping in the night, and their jovial merriments in the daytime*. The devil has *blinded* them as well as *bound* them, and that is one reason of it. But these

cannot on any solid, rational, and religious grounds be freed from the fears of death. But so may the Lord's freemen, and this they have from and through Jesus Christ, (Heb. 2:14-15).

5. Christ will set believers free *from the grave by a joyful resurrection*. That though they come under the stroke and power of death, and are lodged in the grave for a while, yet it shall be but for a while. Death and the grave shall not always have dominion over their body. Death does bind them, but Christ will loose these bonds, and will set them free. As Christ did break the bonds of death, for death was not able to hold him in his grave, (Acts 2:24). So he will knock off the fetters of death from all his, and bring them forth, and make them happy. And this as surely as he himself is risen, (1 Cor. 15:13, *etc.*). And not only free them out of the grave, but also from those evils and imperfections that in this life their bodies are subject to. That though they shall have the same bodies for substance that they have now, yet they shall be better bodies as to the qualities that they then shall have.

1. Then Christ will free them from that *mortality that now they are subject to*. Now liable to death every day and hour, but then they shall die no more forever.

2. Then Christ shall free them *from all pain and sickness*, from cold, and hunger, and thirst they are now often sensible of. Their head shall never ache, their hearts shall never be sick, no part in the least pained to all eternity.

3. Then Christ shall free them *from a necessity of food to sustain them*, and of nourishment from the use of creatures, by which they are repaired and supported daily on this side of the grave, but on the other side of the grave they shall need this no more than the angels do in heaven.

4. Then Christ shall free them *from that weariness that now our bodies often feel, and do groan under.* For he will make them strong and powerful bodies. Nowadays work in the service of God wearies our bodies. But hereafter though they shall be employed through an endless eternity in praising and glorifying of God, they shall neither be weary of it through wickedness nor weary in it through weakness, for as much as Christ will free them from both, (1 Cor. 15:42-43).

5. Christ will then so free them *from all imperfections that they shall be made like to Christ's glorious body.* And can we desire greater freedom for our bodies, than to be make like Christ's glorious body, (Phil. 3:21).

6. Christ does *free all his from the damnation of hell*, that when the devil's captives shall be pained and tormented by exquisite and unspeakable punishment, rolling and tumbling, shrieking and howling, and with bitter cries lamenting themselves, the redeemed of Christ shall never be touched with the flames of that fire. The "second death shall have no power over them," (Rev. 20:6). Christ will take care that those that love him above all and choose him before all shall never come into condemnation, (John 3:16-18). O what mercy this is, to be freed from hell! O what grace and kindness this is to those that were once captives, and had deserved it, and were in danger of it, that by Christ they should be freed and delivered from it! O what mercy would the damned that have felt the pains and punishment of hell, think, say, and confess it to be, if they may be let out and freed from it. But they are in it, and shall never be delivered from it. But the Lord's freemen are out of it, and shall never be cast into it. So great is the liberty we have by Christ the Redeemer of captives, in respect of what we are freed from.

What are the positive blessings that we are free unto by Christ? For Christ came to poor sinners to redeem them when captives, not only that they should not be miserable, but that they should also be *happy*. These things are many and great and glorious. Let me give you a taste in these few.

1. *By Christ believers have freedom and liberty to come to the throne of grace.* A burden to wicked graceless hearts it is, to come and pray to God, they are backward to it, weary of it, as if it were a part of their slavery and bondage, to come and beg for mercy for their souls, for pardon for their sin, for converting and renewing grace now, and for eternal endless glory hereafter. Judge this as you will, yet know it cost Christ dearly to purchase this liberty for us. It is not only a duty that we must, but it is a real privilege that we may have the freedom to come to God on our knees, to beg for special, spiritual, temporal and eternal mercies. Would not a poor prisoner that has deserved to die account it a privilege to have liberty as often as he will, and when he will to have liberty of access to the king, to prefer his petitions to him, and to beg for a pardon of his fact, and for the saving of his life. And all this with hopes of speeding and obtaining what he does petition for? When man had sinned, he was driven out of paradise, and was afraid because of guilt, and there was no freedom for the rebellious sinner without Christ, to come before a provoked angry God with hopes of mercy. But there is a new and living way now found out for you, (Heb. 10:19-22), that you might come with freedom, and ask with freedom of spirit, and with freedom of speech, what Christ has purchased for you, and God has promised to you, (Eph. 3:12; Heb. 4:16). You may with freedom come to God, and tell him all your *grievances*, and all your *burdens*, and all

Chapter 11: Freedom in Christ

your *temptations*, and all that you *lack*, and open all your *heart* to him.

2. By Christ believers have a freedom and a liberty to apply the promises of the gospel to themselves. These promises are *many, great, and precious* promises, of *many, great, and precious* things, and you are free to them all. Not only free to read them, but free to apply them to yourselves, and to live on them, and to wait and hope for the fulfilling and performance of them. Here is a promise of pardon, and it is made to me. A promise, of more grace and of perseverance, and it is made to me, a promise of eternal life and glory, and the blessed glorious God has made it to me, and by Christ I may freely apply it, and build and rest on it.

3. By Christ we are made free to all the privileges of redeemed people. These are also many, great, and precious, very many, very great, and very precious privileges.

1. Believers are free by Christ to a state of friendship and favor with God. As there is a freedom between friends, so there is between God and his redeemed by Christ, that are partakers of the benefits of his redemption, from a state of enmity to a state of friendship and reconciliation. God is no more your enemy, nor you any longer enemies to God. A peace is made by Christ between God and your souls, and this is a firm, and lasting, an everlasting peace, (Col. 1:20-21). Now with comfort you may conclude, though men do hate me, yet God does love me. Though men are my enemies, yet God is my friend, my surest and my fastest friend.

2. By Christ believers are free to a state of justification, the righteousness of Christ is freely imputed to them. That as the devil's captives are under the imputation of Adam's disobedience, so the Lord's freemen are under the imputation of Christ's righteousness and obedience, (Rom. 5:19; 2 Cor. 5:21), and you are free to trust, and to plead the righteousness of Christ for your justification in the sight of God.

3. *By Christ believers are made free to a state of sonship, and the privilege of adoption.* Of slaves you are become not only servants but sons, of the children of the devil, are become the children of God. Of the children of God's wrath, the children of his love. Men may redeem captives, but do not adopt them for their children. But all that Christ redeems have the liberty to become the sons of God, (John 1:12; 2 Cor. 6).

4. *By Christ believers are free to have communion with God in his ordinances.* God is no longer a stranger to them, nor are they any longer strangers to God, but have sweet conversation and fellowship with God, (1 John 1:3). They come to duty, and meet with God in duty, in praying, hearing, and receiving, they have experience of the gracious, powerful, and heart-quickening, and soul-comforting, cheering, softening influences of the Spirit of God, and of the goings forth of their souls in love unto desires after, and delight in God. And when it is so, how sweet is this to their souls!

5. *By Christ believers are free to a right to heaven, and to the enjoyment of the blessed glorious God forever in his kingdom.* They are made free to the happiness of the life to come. They shall have free admission into the heavenly paradise. The gates of heaven shall be set wide open for their departing souls, freely, without any stop or hindrance. They are free in part now, and they shall be perfectly free among the saints in glory when they die, (Rom. 8:21). This glory is prepared for them, (Matt. 25:34). And they are prepared for it, (Rom. 9:23; Col. 1:12). And what your happiness shall be then is beyond the power and ability of any man on earth to declare

fully to you, (1 Cor. 2:8). It might be better done by a glorious angel that is in possession of it, than by a sinful (though sanctified) man, that lives, and waits, and hopes, and prays in expectation of it. Yet the very names by which it is called, might help you to some conceptions of the greatness of its excellency and glory: (1) It is called a *crown*, and that which far surpasses all earthly crowns, (1 Peter 1:4-5), a "crown of life," (James 1:12), a "crown of righteousness," (2 Tim. 4:8), a "crown of glory," (1 Peter 5:4). (2) It is called a "kingdom," (Matt. 25:34). (3) It is called "our Master's joy," (Matt. 25:21, 23). (4) It is called "our Father's house," and the "house of the Father of our Lord Jesus," (John 14:2). (5) It is called "the inheritance of the saints in light," (Col. 1:12). (6) It is the "purchase of Christ," (Eph. 1:14). (7) It is called "eternal life," (Rom. 6:23). Besides these names by which it is called, dwell in your thoughts on one text that sets it forth, until you find your hearts to be affected with it, and long to be possessed of it, and that is 2 Corinthians 4:17, where you observe how the apostle proceeds by steps to come to the top expression of this happiness to which you are made free.

1. It is called *glory*. Now free in *grace*, then in *glory*. The thought of that glory would darken and disgrace the greatest glory of this world.

2. It is called a *weight of glory*, not a burdensome weight, not a weight to weary you, are your afflictions weighty? So shall your glory be, but afflictions are but light, if compared to the weight of glory.

3. It is an *exceeding weight of glory*. It does exceed all worldly glory.

4. It is a *more exceeding weight of glory*, more than can be conceived.

5. It is a *far more exceeding weight of glory.*

6. It is *eternal* too. All this is not for a little while only, or for some thousands of years only, but forever and forever. The glory of the world, as it is but light, if weighed with this. So it is but fading and transitory, and but short, if compared with this that is eternal. Thus you have a little view (and alas it is but little) of the positive freedom and liberty that you have by Christ.

CHAPTER 12: APPLICATION AND USES

Containing the uses of the whole.

Use 1. Then search your hearts, and examine narrowly and thoroughly what you are, bond-men or free, whether yet captives or redeemed and set at liberty. The misery of spiritual captives you have heard does exceed the misery of captives by men. And the good estate of such as are made free by Christ you have also heard. Now say to yourself, *Tell, O my soul, which of these two is your state and your condition. One of them is your condition, but which it is worthy of your strictest search, and most diligent inquiry. Are your fetters knocked off, and your bonds broken, and your chain cut, and you delivered? Or are you yet held fast by them? Take heed, O my soul, of being mistaken in this point. If you take it for granted that you are made free, when yet you are in bonds, and leave your body in this mistake, you are lost forever. If on the other hand you say you are still a captive, when you are made free, you will lose the comfort of your freedom, and will spend your time and life in complaints, and griefs, and fears, which you should spend in praising and admiring God for his love and mercy in bringing you out of your captivity.*

For your help in this, take these few marks to try yourselves by for the resolution of this question.

1. *Freemen have their spiritual eyesight restored to them.* When Christ opens the prison doors to let the captives out, he does also open their eyes, to let them see that in sin, in God, in Christ, in grace and holiness that they never saw before. That the redeemed captive cries out, O I never thought my heart had been so bad, so bad, so very bad as now I see it is. I never thought that sin had been so vile, so very vile, and so

deformed as now I plainly see it is. I never thought that Christ was so excellent, and so necessary, so absolutely necessary for me, as I now see he is. O I think he is now altogether lovely, altogether desirable. After I have had a view of the beauty and the excellency of Christ, I think all the glory of the world, and all the delights in pleasure and sin is darkened, and does vanish and disappear. O how I was blinded in my captivity, that I never saw the excellency of Christ, and deformity of sin until now, (Isa. 42:6; Acts 26:18, 23; Col. 1:13; Rev. 3:18).

2. *When Christ breaks the bonds by which poor captives were held, he also breaks their hearts that they have been kept and held by it in the service of Satan and sin, from God and Christ so long.* As the eye does see and weep, so the heart does consider, and bleed, and grieve at the remembrance of his former folly and sin. O what did I do to sin against this blessed, gracious, merciful God! O what did I mean so long to stop my ears against all the calls, and wooings, and entreatings of this Lord-Redeemer, who was so kind to suffer, bleed, and die for such a wretch as I, for such a rebellious, disobedient, and delaying wretch as I. O there is no love like his, there is no mercy like his, there is no kindness like his! O why did I slight him so much, so long, so very much, so very long as I have done? O what a fool I was, to prefer the world, the pleasures and the profits of the world, before this blessed Redeemer! O what a beast I was, to prefer my very lusts and sins, and the service of the devil, before this glorious, gracious Savior, and the serving of him that died to deliver me from my bondage! O Lord I am grieved that I ever did so. It is the burden and breaking of my heart that I ever did so. O now I could wash myself in tears at the remembrance of my folly and my madness! But if I should, that will not wash me from my guilt, and from my filth. And

because that would not do, this blessed Savior shed his blood for the cleansing of me from my guilt and my pollution. I weep, but not enough. My heart is troubled, but not enough. My soul is humbled within me, but not enough, for such great rebellion against, and slighting of this Lord Redeemer. But I am troubled because I am no more troubled. Lord I grieve, because my heart is yet so hard, and can grieve no more. My sin is bitter to me now, which once was sweet and pleasant to my soul.

3. *Such as are made free by Christ are delivered from the reigning power of sin.* For it is impossible to be a willing voluntary servant of sin, and yield obedience to the law of sin, and to be made free by Christ, (2 Peter 2:19; Rom. 6:16, 18). Does sin command you, and you obey? Does sin have the chiefest room and place in your affections and your hearts? If so, you are then yet in your bondage.

4. *Such as are made free by Christ have resigned up themselves, their hearts, their love, their all to him,* receive *him as Lord as well as for their Savior, and to consent to take him in all his offices, for prophet, priest, and king,* and giving up themselves to him, do become his servants and consequently yield obedience to him. They have changed their master, and they have changed their work and ways, and are become new creatures, having new hearts, wills, and affections, ends and designs, than what they had before. For the condition of sinners being partakers of Christ's redemption is their believing on him, and consenting to him as Lord and Savior, choosing him before all, and loving him above all, and if you do not do this you are yet in your bondage to Satan and sin.

For is it not reasonable that you should be the servants of him who brings you from this slavery? And if he purchases and buys you out, is it not reasonable that you should take him for your Lord, and obey him? And that *universally*, submitting to all his laws, even those that are most spiritual, and cross to your corrupt hearts and most beloved sins, not pick and choose, but to have respect to them all, (Psa. 119:6), *constantly*, not by fits and starts, not only when in straits and sickness, but at all times to have the frame, and bent, and inclination of your hearts to yield obedience to Christ, your Lord-Redeemer, *freely and voluntarily*, as matter of your choice, from a free principle of love, because you love him, you will pray to him. Because you love him, you will hear from him, and wait and attend on him, rejoicing when you please him, grieving when you do offend him.

If by these things you discover what you are, bond or free, I shall close the whole with an exhortation to both sorts, *both bond and free*.

Use of *exhortation*, 1. *To you that are bound, that you would look after spiritual freedom*. Young men that have hard service, long to be made free, and those that are in prisons and chains, long to be at liberty, and shall any of you be content to abide in your thralldom? What will sin do for you? And what will Satan do for you, that you are so unwilling to leave their service? Has the Redeemer come, and will you not mind him? Has he paid the ransom, and waits for your response of him, and will you still refuse him, and the liberty and freedom you may have by him, and cannot have without him? What do you say, sirs, you young and old? Shall I have your answers? Will you be made free, or will you continue in your bondage? If you will, you may. Be but willing, and your chain shall be taken from you. If you will not remember liberty was offered to you, and you did refuse it, you would not be free. Though you have

Chapter 12: Application and Uses

been a very vile sinner, and rebellious, yet you may be made free, (Psa. 68:18; Isa. 49:6). Do these *things:*

1. *Labor to convince yourself that you were born in bondage, a slave by nature to Satan and sin.* The Pharisees did not believe that they were in bondage, and therefore did not look out to Christ to be made free, (John 8:33). This is the undoing of multitudes, that they conclude their condition to be good, when it is not so, and they conclude before they try. Did you but see your bonds, and understand your slavery, ministers would have hopes that by their sermons they may do you good.

2. *Work on your heart by serious consideration, your misery and deplorable condition while you are in a state of bondage.* When by diligent search you have found yourself in a bondage condition, hold your thoughts to this subject until you are awakened and affected with it. Think with yourself, and say, O my soul! Being yet a captive to Satan and to sin, you are yet an enemy to God, a slighter of Christ, under the guilt of all your sin, in danger of damnation. Awake, arise, and look about you, and get out of this condition, lest it be too late forever.

3. *Set yourself under the preaching of the word, and constantly attend on God, and come to the hearing of the word, as to an ordinance of God.* And look on faithful ministers as the ambassadors of Jesus Christ, that come to you in the name of Christ, as having authority from God to propose the gospel conditions of deliverance from captivity, and to treat with you in the name of God about your being made free. So indeed it is in 2 Corinthians 5:19-20. You come to hear a man's parts, but you do not look on them as persons *in office*, having a commission from God to propound articles of peace between God and you, to treat with you from God, and in the name of God, about your everlasting state, and your deliverance from

your present bondage, and future torment. Did you believe this, would you sit and sleep as if what were delivered to you were not worth the hearing and regarding? Or would you sit and hear, and go away and slight all that has been said to you?

4. *Make application of the word of God, when you hear it, to yourselves.* This is spoken to me, this is my misery, and this is my condition, and this is my danger, and merely offered to sinners, is offered to me, and Christ is tendered to me to help me out of my woeful state of bondage. The minister makes uses of the doctrine he delivers, but all this is ineffectual until you take it and lay it home to your own hearts. For lack of this, you sit and hear like people not concerned. You sit and hear without affection, and go away without the due and powerful effect of the Word on your hearts. Let conscience tell you, you are the drunkard, the hypocrite, the unbeliever, that is threatened and in danger of damnation.

5. *Look up to God through the ordinance, and beyond the minister that does speak to your ear, that God would speak to your heart and conscience.* Ministers might speak, and yet conscience might not speak. Minister and conscience might both speak, conscience seconding the minister that says you are in a dreadful condition while you are in spiritual bondage. Yes, says conscience too, so you are. And yet until God shall speak, you will not hearken. O then when you come to the place where sinners are made free, look up to God that he would speak to your hearts.

6. *Pray to God that he would have mercy on you, and pity you in your bondage, and help you out.* As a poor prisoner, look through the grates to heaven, and say, *Lord, some pity for a poor prisoner, some relief and help for a poor captive. Lord, I am in chains of sin, but cannot break them, held fast by Satan,*

Chapter 12: Application and Uses

O do not let me perish. O do not let me live and die in the spiritual bondage. I give myself to you, on my knees, I do resign myself, my will, my love, my heart, and all to you. Sinner, will you when you come home, not sit and talk vainly, and not sit idly as heretofore, but go apart, and beg of God for mercy, and do it earnestly. For it is for your life, your soul.

2. Exhortation: *To you that are set at liberty.* Your privilege is a singular privilege, and calls for something singular from you. You were debtors to God, and prisoners to his justice, and were liable to everlasting punishment in the life to come. But Christ has made you free, and you are free indeed, (John 8:36). Stir up and awaken yourselves to these following duties.

First, *be thankful to God and Christ*, that of bond-men you are made free. If a captive was delivered out of Turkish slavery by the means of another, or a man exposed to a perpetual imprisonment for his debt, another should free him from the prison, and the dangers thereof. What expressions of thankfulness would he abundantly utter, saying, *O sir, I owe my present ease, and freedom from my future danger, to you. I shall never forget your kindness while I live. I do acknowledge I do not have another such friend that has done the like for me in the entire world.* For as much then as the difference of being a debtor to God, and a debtor to man, of being exposed to a prison on earth, and to the prison of hell, is unspeakably great, and I think you should break forth into holy admirations of the grace and love of God, and say, *O Lord, I was indebted to you in the debt of sin, and of that I am discharged and freed. And now I am indebted in the debt of thankfulness to you. O the riches of this grace! O the greatness of this love and favor! Was love ever like this? Was any kindness ever comparable to the kindness and the bounty which you have showed to my soul?*

O Lord, I am forced to cry out, I never had, and never can have in heaven or in earth, such another friend as you have been and are to my soul!

But alas, O Lord, I find my heart exceedingly dull and dead. A smaller kindness from a fellow creature would have greatly affected me, and have made deep impressions on my heart. But by sad experience, and to the grieving of my soul, I find, I am too *too* stupid and insensible of this manifest and matchless mercy, which you have freely vouchsafed to me! I believe that there are many now in the hellish prison, as certainly as if I saw them with my eyes, where I also might have been. And I see others in this world still captives to the devil, fast bound in the cords and chains of lust and sin that are going to the place of that cursed damned crew of lost souls, eternally separated from the enjoyment of your blessed majesty, among whom you have given me good hope through grace that I shall never be. You show mercy to me, while you pour out your wrath and fury on them. O where is this! And how does this come to pass? Why am I, a poor silly wr*etc*h, a partaker of this love? What did you see in me but filth and sin, that might have provoked you to deal with me as you have done with them? Surely, Lord, you had mercy on me because you would have mercy on me! When I did lie in my blood, and bonds, in my fetters and my chains of sin and guilt, you did pass by me, but did not pass me by, but showed grace and goodness to me! When your servant and apostle Peter was in prison, bound in chains, and the keepers before the door kept the prison, you did send your angel, who came to him, and a light shined in the prison, and he said to him, *arise up quickly*, and his chains fell off from his hands. But when I was in a worse case, and sorer condition, having fetters on my soul, and darkness in my understanding, and the devil the keeper of the prison stood to watch me, to keep me in his stronghold, you did send your Son (for an angle could not do it) to knock off the chains by which I was held, and your Spirit came on me, and a light did shine into my mind, and he said, arise up quickly, and the chains fell off from my soul. All this you did for me, a captive and a prisoner, and it was long before I knew that it was true which was done for me. But while I think and muse hereon, how I was bound, and now am set at liberty. How I was enthralled, and in great distress, and you have enlarged me. I begin to find and feel my love to kindle in my breast, and my heart to be enlarged with your praise, and as your apostle did sit in the prison and sing, so shall my soul, being brought forth and delivered from captivity, magnify your name. Come then, awake O my soul! Triumph and sing, be glad, and greatly rejoice, since your loving, holy, blessed Lord has opened the prison doors, and brought you forth into the liberty of the sons of God. Oh! "Bless the Lord, O my soul, and all that is within me, bless his Holy Name. Bless the Lord, O my soul, and do not forget all his benefits, who forgives all your iniquities, who heals all your diseases, who redeems your life from destruction, who crowns you with lovingkindness and tender mercies."

To quicken your hearts to real thankfulness for deliverance from this bondage, and captivity, dwell in your thoughts on these following particulars.

1. *The greatness of your debt for which you were exposed to everlasting imprisonment.* Consider here the kinds of your sins, the number and the aggravations of them.

2. *Work on your thoughts, your utter inability and incapacity to make payment of your debt,* for want of which you might have been a prisoner forever. You could not say to

God as the servant did to his fellow servant that demanded his debt of him, "Have patience with me, and I will pay you all," (Matt. 18:29). There was a double debt that you owed to God, one as a reasonable creature, the other as an unreasonable sinner. The first was the debt of obedience required by the Law, the other the debt of punishment for the transgression of the Law. And you have paid neither of them, not the debt of perfect and perpetual obedience. First, because all that you can do is due for the present, and that which is due for the present will not be accepted as payment for that which is past, as if a tenant owes for rent, due many quarters past, the payment of the rent due from the last quarter will not satisfy for all that was due before. Secondly, all that you could do is less than what you ought to do. And in strict justice a part of payment is not accepted for the whole. Every living man comes far short of his duty to God, and runs more and more in arrears with God, and therefore so far from paying that we run daily behind hand. Thirdly, man in bondage did not have the least mite of that kind which the law requires and accepts, in other words, sinless, spotless, and perfect obedience without mixture of sin, pure gold without any dross. And if the prisoner offers for his liberty money that is not current, the creditor may refuse it, and keep him in the prison still. And you could not pay the debt of obedience to the Law, so neither could you satisfy for the debt of punishment due to you for your disobedience thereunto. The payment or satisfaction must be equivalent to the wrong that was done. God that was offended is an infinite God. Therefore, that which satisfies that the offender might be free, must be something of an infinite value, which no mere man has to give to God. And therefore, those prisoners that are not set free by Christ shall be always paying, but can never fully pay;

satisfying, but can never fully satisfy; and therefore such shall never be released, but must lie in prison forever.

Thirdly, weigh this also, *satisfaction must be made, or the prisoner will never have his liberty.* God might, and did demand his debt. When Adam sinned, *hue and cry* was made after the offender. *Adam, where are you?* was apprehended and arraigned at the bar, *what have you done?* Have you eaten of the fruit of the tree, of which I commanded that you should not eat? He was convicted by his own confession, *I did eat,* and was condemned and a sad sentence past unto him, (Gen. 3:17-19). This was the pitiful case that man was in, he had sinned, he was apprehended, found guilty, under sentence, justice required satisfaction. Man could not give it, and thus he did not know which way to turn himself for help and for deliverance from his bondage and captivity which by sin he had brought himself to. O what a straight you were in, when you owed millions, and did not have one mite to pay? After you have prayed on this, *consider,*

Fourthly, *to release you from your bonds Jesus Christ did voluntarily undertake for you, did interpose himself between the wrath of God and the poor captive, enthralled sinner, as if Christ should say, Father, man that was made free, has abused his liberty and is become a bond-slave, fallen into the hands of revenging justice, which might arrest him, and clap him up in prison forever. I see he is undone and lost. He cannot help himself, but I will be his surety and his bail. What he owes you, set that on my account, I will pay it. I am willing to do and suffer in their nature what may please and satisfy your justice. If my life will be taken for their salvation, I will lay it down, if my blood will be accepted for the ransom of these poor prisoners I will shed it for them, rather than that they should always remain in this captivity.* O can you think how ready Christ was to engage, and to become your surety to die for you, that you might live, to be bound for you, that your bonds might be broken, and your soul escapes, and not have your heart affected with his love, and your tongue employed in his praises? "Who is this that engaged his heart to approach to me? says the Lord," (Jer. 30:21). Who is this forward engager, that is so willing and hearty in this work? It is one that is able and mighty to save, to redeem by price and power, poor captive sinners, even the only Son of the ever blessed God, and so he is said to be our surety, (Heb. 7:22). A surety is one that undertakes for, or gives assurance in the behalf of another. One entering into a bond and standing engaged for another to do and to perform for another, what he was bound to do. Among men suretiship is a dangerous thing. He that is surety for another un-insures his own estate. "He that is surety for a stranger shall smart for it, and he that hates suretiship is sure," (Prov. 11:15). But notwithstanding, suretiship is in this way among men, yet Christ would become a surety for us to God himself, to bring us forth from our bondage. And that you might be the more affected, and enflamed with his love, consider how far he acted for poor captives beyond whatever man did for any man.

1. *How many captives Christ engages for!* How many millions he became a surety for, for their ransom and deliverance! One man might be bound, and become a surety for one, or two, but who will be surety for thousands? Especially if you *add,*

2. *The greatness of the debt of those he became a surety for.* One man might be persuaded to be surety for another, if the debt is small. But if it is for thousands and for millions, men are

shy, but if it is for multitudes that owe such great sums, everyone so much, who will be persuaded to be surety for them? But if they are in prison or in bondage there, they lie for want of money of their own, or suretiship from another. But Christ became surety for multitudes, and each one owed inbundance, that it does pass the skill of the ablest arithmetician to cast up the total sum that one of these prisoners was in bondage for.

3. *Christ most certainly knew that he should pay undoubtedly the debt of all he became a surety for.* Many men are sureties for others, hoping they shall never be called on for the debt, but that the debtor will pay it himself. Some will be bound for a man, whom they judge to be worth as much as they owe and more too. But if it is a poor man, not worth one farthing, and his debt is thousands, who will then become surety for him? He is a prisoner, and so he is like to be. And if any become bound for another, and pay the debt for him, what trouble does this cause to him? It breaks his sleep and he is displeased with himself, that he ever entered into a bond, and says it shall be a warning to me, while I live, how I become a surety for another. I thought him able enough, else I would not have brought myself into such snares.

But all this was known to Christ, when he did become our surety. He knew our beggary and our poverty, and that we could not contribute the smallest mite, towards the satisfaction to be made in order to the freeing of the captives from their bondage, and he knew that God would not spare him, but exact the utmost from him. And yet he did voluntarily undertake our ransom. O what love was this!

4. *Christ became a surety for you, when you were a stranger to him.* He did undertake to release you out of your bonds and fetters when you had no special actual relation to

him. Some men will not be sureties for their most intimate acquaintance, and near relations, not for a brother, father, son, but for a stranger who will do it? In this then admire the love of Christ that when you were in chains of sin and guilt, and a stranger too, Christ did undertake and did pay a ransom for you.

5. Yet more to affect your heart, consider, *that Christ did ransom you from your captivity when you were an enemy to him*. A man might possibly take some pity on a stranger, but an enemy that hates him, and that would and does dishonor and reproach him, who would be deeply engaged for him? Yet Christ did this for you, when you were enemies to Christ, (Rom. 5:10).

6. Yet to raise your admiration and affection more, consider *Christ did become a surety for you, before you did or could desire any such kindness at his hands*. What man or angel could have thought of the ransoming of captives by the Son of God, becoming the Son of man, and God himself redeem us by his blood? How long might you ask, how many might you go to? And how many entreaties might you use before you can prevail with one to be engaged for you so much, when you have nothing of your own? But Christ did this for us all, before any man had any such desire in his heart, thought in his mind, request in his mouth, that he would do so great and wonderful a kindness for us.

7. *Christ did this alone, without any other engaging with him*. Men require counter-security. If I am bound for you (says one) you shall find another to be bound with me, to be bound for me, to save me harmless. Or you shall make over such houses, or such lands for my security, that if I am called on, or the bond be put in suit against me, I might save myself. But as

Christ did tread the winepress of God's wrath alone, so did he alone undertake to ransom and redeem us from our bondage and captivity.

8. *Christ never repented of this undertaking, nor desired to stand bound no longer.* Men engaged for others, when they fear they will fail, make all the means they can to get out of the bond, and to stand surety no longer. They will scarce sleep until they get themselves free, though the party that is the principal debtor is arrested and put in prison. But Jesus Christ our Lord-Redeemer and surety, to bring us out of bondage was constant to the death. And when Peter did dissuade him from suffering (which was the payment of our ransom), how sharply did Christ rebuke him, (Matt. 6:21-23)? Yes, he was desirous of the time of actual performance, "I have a baptism to be baptized with, and how I am strained until it is accomplished," (Luke 12:50). Christ never said, I repent that I ever undertook to ransom captive sinners. God indeed said that he repented that he made man, (Gen. 6:6), but Christ never repented that he had engaged himself to redeem sinners.

9. *Consider what it was that was the price that Christ gave to make you free from your captivity.* Men might be surety for men to pay a sum of money, but Christ became our surety to the shedding of his own most precious blood. Men might give some money to redeem a captive from Turkish slavery. But Christ gave himself, his life, his soul and body, to bring us from our bitter bondage, and miserable captivity. So take some time to ponder on the Lord, your surety that did so freely undertake the ransoming of your captive souls. Which was the fourth head to get your hearts affected with this privilege of being set at liberty.

Fifthly, consider, *That God was pleased to accept of the undertaking of Christ, and what he has laid down for your ransom from captivity.* God might have exacted the debt from man that did owe it. It is a voluntary act for a man to become a surety, no man is to be compelled to it. And it is a voluntary act of the creditor to accept such a surety, they are both free and at their choice. But when the one offers himself to become bound, and the other does accept of his suretiship, then the debtor or prisoner is relieved.

It was free love in Christ to become our Redeemer. It was grace in God to accept Christ's ransom for us. The Son might have said, *Man has sinned, why should I suffer? Man has deserved the wrath of God, let him undergo it.* And the Father might have said, *Man has transgressed my law, and violated my covenant, and I will make him suffer for it. They have brought themselves into bonds of misery, and they shall lie therein, and they that sinned, themselves shall die.* O wonder then at this blessed agreement between the Father and the Son, for the bringing forth of poor souls in bondage from their captivity.

Seventhly, from all the former it follows, *the salvation of such as are made free is sure and certain.* Heaven now belongs to you, and you have a title to the glory above. Does Satan object against you, that you have sinned, and deserved to lie in everlasting chains, you might reply: it is true, but Christ is my surety and redeemer, and has set me free. Does the Law or conscience accuse you, might answer all from the ransom of your Redeemer. Do you fear the justice of God, why your debt is paid by your surety, and then the debtor cannot be cast into prison. The surety and the debtor in law are but one person, and the surety is liable to make satisfactory payment, (Prov. 22:26-27), and Christ has done it, and you discharged.

God has given some to Christ, whom he is to bring to heaven. And they shall not perish, (John 6:38-40), as Judah did engage Jacob for Benjamin, "I will be surety for him, of my hands you shall require him: if I do not bring him to you, and set him before you, then let me bear the blame forever," (Gen. 43:9). And therefore when Benjamin was to be detained by Joseph, Judah pleads hard, and offers himself to abide in his stead and to be a bond-man there, so that Benjamin might return to his father with his brothers, (Gen. 44:33). Christ has undertaken to bring all those out of their bonds and fetters, which the Father gave to him, and to set them in heaven before him. The price is paid, the bonds are broken, the chains fallen from your souls, in which you were held while unconverted. As he has opened the prison doors that you might come forth, so he will open to you the palace gates that you may enter in. For hopes hereof be thankful, be exceedingly thankful and rejoice in the Lord your Redeemer.

Second *exhortation*. The next duty I would press on you *is to be compassionate and to put on tender bowels of pity toward those that are yet bound in the fetters and chains of their sin and guilt*. While you do rejoice in that you are free, do not forget to commiserate those that are yet captives.

1. *Let ministers think of this* when they are studying for, and praying for, and preaching to their people, how they are in bondage and in slavery, and that unless their chains are loosed and their fetters broken and knocked off, their souls are lost forever. And that they will be faster shortly bound hand and foot and cast into a place of outer and eternal darkness. Some serious and believing thoughts of their present danger, and their future misery would put more life into all we do for their recovery and prevention of their everlasting condemnation.

Should we then preach to them with such lukewarmness, as if we were telling them a tale, or saying such things in that manner, as if we did not believe, receive and obey the message we deliver to them or not? When they are yet the great and weighty truths of everlasting life or death, to preach a Redeemer to captive souls what skill and life, and love does it require? What zeal and pity to their souls does it call for? O that God would pardon the want of these in me, give me that belief of their eternal state and seriousness of heart that I may ever speak and preach the doctrine of redemption to enslaved sinners, as to those that are undone forever, except they are prevailed with to come to him, submit to him, receive of him, and give up themselves to be his *wholly*, and to be his *only* that has paid the ransom for their deliverance. When some years since I was called occasionally to preach to the prisoners in Newgate, and I saw my hearers come in fetters, and heard their chains rattling at their heels, I thought that it was an affecting spectacle to see men before me that were shortly to be called to the bar of men, and be tried for their lives, and some likely to be sentenced to death and put to execution. But if we do behold our hearers standing before us, though free from such material chains of iron, yet bound fast in their lusts and sins, and consider that they must be shortly tried at the bar of God, and if not delivered by Christ must receive a sentence of death, banished from the presence of the blessed God, cast down to devils and damned Spirits, it should move us to pray for them, weep over them, and preach to them with great pity and compassion. To stand and view so many persons, among whom many are the devil's captives, whom he is leading fettered to eternal perdition, should raise in our hearts strong workings of affections towards them, and speak to them with that earnestness and tender love, as becomes those that are speaking in the name of God to lost sinners in order to their recovery and deliverance from captivity.

2. *Let parents that are made free pity and have compassion on their children that are yet bound.* If any of your children should be laid in irons for some fact committed against the laws of men, and carried bound to execution, would this not pierce your very hearts like a sword, and be a matter of grief and trouble to you? Would not tears flow plentifully from your eyes, and bitter lamentations from your mouth that you should ever bring forth and bring up children that should end their days in such reproach and infamy to you and them? Or if any of you had a son abroad, and you should hear he was taken captive by the Turks, or were in the Spanish Inquisition, what shedding of tears! What wringing of hands! What smiting on your breast would these tidings make! What dolorous complaints and grievous moans would you make, saying, *O my son, my son, my poor afflicted and distressed son, you are fallen into the hands of barbarous and cruel men. You are put to drudgery and slavery! O my son, my son, what shall I do for you, my son? O that I could give or find a ransom for him! If all I have would set him free, he should not lie in chains and fetters, nor continue in that sore captivity!* Why, you parents! Would you so lament the misery of your children's body, and do you make nothing of the misery of your children's souls? Would you in this way take on, and grieve and mourn for their outward bondage, which is consistent with the good condition of their souls, and will shortly have an end, and yet is it nothing to you, to see them in their spiritual bondage, captivated by Satan, and in danger of being cast into an everlasting dungeon of black and thick darkness! O why do you not speak to them, and tell them

of their misery and their remedy, how they came into this condition, and how they may get out of it? Why do you not plead with them, instruct them, and exhort them day and night that they may escape the torments of hell hereafter by being brought out of their bondage now? Why do you not pray to God that he would make them free? Why do you not plead at the throne of grace, and say, *Lord, I have children that are Satan's captives, my poor children are fast bound in fetters of sins, in the bonds of iniquity. O God of grace, that has showed favor to me, show favor to my children also! O that they may be released! O that you would please pity them in their bondage, and for the ransom of your Son let them be redeemed, and by the powerful workings of your Spirit have their wills subdued, and inclined to receive the only Redeemer. Him you did send to proclaim liberty to captives, O that by your grace you would cause them to come in, and lay hold on the mercy granted in the proclamation of the gospel, that they might not perish in their bonds.*

3. *Let masters that are made free and set at liberty have compassion on their servants that are fettered in their chains of sin.* They are not only bound to you (to be so bound is in order to their good and their freedom), but are also bound in the cords of their iniquity, which is their present slavery, and tends to their eternal misery. Does it not pity you, to see your servants, to be servants of the devil, and in bondage to their lusts? Do your hearts not work within you to consider that any under your roof should be drudges to Satan? Or do you see this, and have nothing to say to them all the week long, to make them apprehensive of their danger, and sensible of their misery? Is it enough for you to teach them the skill and art of your trade, and at the expiration of seven years to make them free, while

Chapter 12: Application and Uses

you do neglect to help them (as instruments under God) out of the thralldom of Satan and of sin? Or can it satisfy you that they have at the end of their service to you the *freedom* of the city or corporation where you and they do dwell, while they are not brought into the liberty of the Sons of God? Or can you have peace in the neglect of your duty, to think they came into your family bond-slaves to sin, and after seven year's time, they go out as they came in? Or should you not endeavor that they may be spiritually free, while they continue servants to you? O how would they have cause to bless God for you, and that they ever came within your doors, and dwelt within your walls, if they may say, when I first became a servant to my master, I was a servant to my lusts also, but by his instructions, admonitions, and example, I became a servant of God, before I ceased to be a servant to him? If it should be otherwise, let it not be through your neglect, for as it will not be without sin and misery to your servants, so neither will it be without guilt on you.

The like I might urge on other relations, acquaintances and friends, husbands to have compassion on their wives, wives on their husbands, one neighbor on another. You that know what it is to be made free, do your utmost to help and succor them that are in chains of sin, and do not know the evil of it, nor the good of the contrary condition, and therefore do not mourn under the one, nor desire to be brought forth into the other.

Third *exhortation. Were you in bonds, and are they broken? In fetters, and are they knocked off? Then walk in the whole course of your lives as becomes a ransomed and redeemed people.* It will not become you to live and act as others do. As there is a wonderful difference between your condition, and the condition of others, so there must be, between your conversation and the conversation of others. See that you are humble, holy, heavenly. See that you are fruitful in every good work, faithful to your Lord-Redeemer, and be no more entangled with those sins and snares you were delivered from. Now you are enlarged, walk close with God, holy strictness is the greatest and truest liberty. "I will walk in liberty, for I seek your precepts," (Psa. 119:45). Remember he that has called you to liberty, does not give you leeway to live licentiously, but to tread in the paths of piety. Go on then, hold on your way, continue and persevere therein to the end, and when the servants of sin, at the coming of death, and the day of judgment, shall be bound in a place of darkness, pain, and torment, you shall be free in a place, a palace of rest and light, of life and love, singing, sounding forth the everlasting praises of your Redeemer. *Amen.*

FINIS

Other Books Published by Puritan Publications

The Covenant of Works and the Covenant of Grace – by Edmund Calamy (1600-1666)

The Christian's Combat Against the Devil - Christopher Love (1618-1651)

The Believer's Privileges in the Covenant of Grace - Thomas Watson (1620-1686)

The Lord's Voice Cries to the City: A Biblical Guide for Hearing the Word of God Preached - by C. Matthew McMahon

Christ Inviting Sinners to Come to Him for Rest - by Jeremiah Burroughs (1599-1646)

The Duty of Reformation in Light of God's Mercies - by Thomas Gouge (1605-1681)

A Comfort for the Afflicted Christian - by William Plumer (1802-1880)

A Glimpse of God's Glory - Thomas Hodges (1600-1672)

God's Just Desertion of the Unjust, and Other Works - by Hannibal Gammon (1585-1674)

The Christian's Union, Communion and Conformity to Jesus Christ In His Death and Resurrection - by John Brinsley (1600-1665)

www.ingramcontent.com/pod-product-compliance
Lightning Source LLC
Chambersburg PA
CBHW031956080426
42735CB00007B/419